The Three Nephites

AND OTHER TRANSLATED BEINGS

The Three Nephites

AND OTHER TRANSLATED BEINGS

b y

Bruce E. Dana

BONNEVILLE BOOKS™

Springville, Utah

ISBN: 1-55517-687-9
e.1

Published by Bonneville Books
Imprint of Cedar Fort Inc.
www.cedarfort.com

Distributed by:

Typeset by Kristin Nelson
Cover design by Nicole Cunningham
Cover design © 2003 by Lyle Mortimer

Printed in the United States of America
10 9 8 7 6 5 4 3 2 1

Printed on acid-free paper

Library of Congress Cataloging-in-Publication Data

Dana, Bruce E.
 The three Nephites and other translated beings / by Bruce E. Dana.
    p. cm.
Includes bibliographical references.
 ISBN 1-55517-687-9 (pbk. : alk. paper)
 1. Nephites. 2. Translation to heaven--Mormon Church. I. Title.
 BX8627.D36 2003
 289.3'22--dc21
                    2003000791

Table of Contents

Preface

Though there have been many translated beings, none seem to have captured the interest and intrigue of the Latter-day Saint people as have the Three Nephites. As it pertains to these special men, these questions naturally arise: By what means did they become translated beings? What was their purpose in becoming translated beings? As translated beings, how do they differ from mortals and resurrected beings? Will they ever taste of death? Through the scriptures, and the words of General Authorities, this work will address these searching questions.

In addition to the Three Nephites, this work will talk about other translated beings—Enoch, Melchizedek, Moses, Elijah, John the Beloved, Alma the younger, and Nephi, who is the son of the third Helaman. Though not classified as a translated being, this work will also discuss the cursed individual, Cain, who is still alive and was seen twice by Elder David W. Patten.

Translated beings are special individuals with special powers and abilities. With this introduction, let us begin our fascinating study of the translated beings, the Three Nephites.

Acknowledgments

Though I have written this introduction in each of my previous books, it is important to emphasize that without the support of my wife, Brenda, this work would never have been written. Only those who write books, and especially doctrinal works, know of the tremendous amount of time involved in researching and writing them. Writers are born with a desire to write and I am grateful that my family allows me time to fulfill this desire.

I am thankful for all of my children: Janalene, Connie, Michelle, Tami, Heather, Brooke, Benjamin and Nathan; my parents, Edward and Shirley Dana, and my wife's parents, Max and Jody Lamb, for their constant love and devotion.

I am especially grateful for Lee Nelson, Lyle Mortimer, and Chad Daybell of Cedar Fort, Inc., for their confidence in publishing my previous books. I express my appreciation to the staff of Cedar Fort—for their friendship and help in performing all of the necessary details that produce a professional and marketable product.

In writing this work, I am very grateful for my dear friend, Dennis "C" Davis, who, for thirty years, has generously shared his vast knowledge of the gospel with me, and has reviewed my writings so they will be doctrinally correct. There are other friends, Jean Britt, Donald Speth, and Vaughn Cook, who have taken the time to read all or a portion of my manuscript and given valuable comments and suggestions.

Chapter One

In the Land Bountiful
(3 Nephi 8: 5; 10: 18; 11: 1-15; Alma 22: 29)

One of the most inspiring events written in the *Book of Mormon* is the appearance of the resurrected Lord to about twenty-five hundred men, women, and children, "in the land Bountiful," as recorded in Third Nephi. Chosen from among this blessed multitude were the Nephite Twelve. "Chapter 28," of Third Nephi, says Dr. Sidney B. Sperry,[1] "deals almost entirely with promises of their heart's desire which Jesus made to each of the Twelve, and more especially with three of their number who were given the assurance that they should live to bring souls to Him and behold all the doings of the Father unto the children of men until Christ should come in His glory."[2]

Dr. Sperry has further written that Mormon, the great historian, "explains that the Three had a change wrought upon their bodies so that they could not die; in this state they were to remain until the judgment day of Christ, at which time they were to undergo a greater change and be received into the kingdom of the Father. They were to suffer no pain or sorrow except for the sins of the world; the Evil One, Mormon points out, was to have no power over them whatever, and the powers of the earth could not hold them."[3]

There are many interesting stories that have been

circulated among the Latter-day Saint people concerning appearances of these three ancient men in modern times. A few of these will be mentioned later in this work. We begin our study of the Three Nephites by learning of events that transpired in their lives and enthused them with the desire to remain on the earth.

Many members of the Church have concluded that the resurrected Lord appeared to the Nephite multitude following the three days of destruction and darkness upon the land. To help clarify when this dramatic event took place, we again rely upon Dr. Sperry for knowledge: "In verse 18 of chapter 10 Mormon anticipated the appearance of the resurrected Christ to His people, by pointing to the fact that He came apparently at the 'ending of the thirty-fourth year.' A comparison of this verse with 8: 5 will show that nearly a year passed by after the great three days of darkness and destruction before our Lord appeared to the Nephites. This conclusion is borne out by a careful study of other facts in the record as written by Mormon."[4]

In a footnote, he wrote this explanation: "Notice, for example, that at the end of the first day's ministry (19: 1-3) of the Savior to the Nephites, the people go casually to their homes and even know where to find their friends. This settled condition could scarcely have existed immediately following the great destruction at the time of the Savior's death."[5]

In harmony with Dr. Sperry's comments regarding the time of the appearance of the resurrected Lord, Elder Bruce R. McConkie[6] says: "The Nephites adjusted their calendar so as to begin a new dating era with the birth of Jesus; and according to their chronology, the storms and the darkness and the crucifixion came to pass on the fourth day of the first month of the thirty-fourth year (3 Ne. 8). Then 'in the ending' of that year (3 Ne. 10: 18-19), several months after the Ascension on Olivet [in Jerusalem], Jesus ministered personally among the Nephites for many hours on many days."[7]

As the Nephite multitude were "conversing about this Jesus Christ, of whom the sign had been given concerning his death," they heard a "voice as if it came out of heaven." Their frames quaked, and their hearts burned as the "small voice" pierced them to the soul. They also heard the voice a second time without understanding it. The third time, they understood "the voice which they heard," that said: "Behold my Beloved Son, in whom I am well pleased, in whom I have glorified my name—hear ye him."

After the congregation "cast their eyes up again towards heaven," they saw a "Man descending out of heaven" clothed in "a white robe." He came down and "stood in the midst of them." The people did not know "what it meant, for they thought it was an angel that had appeared unto them." After stretching "forth his hand," he declared: "Behold, I am Jesus Christ, whom the prophets testified shall come into the world. And behold, I am the light and the life of the world; and I have drunk out of that bitter cup which the Father hath given me, and have glorified the Father in taking upon me the sins of the world, in the which I have suffered the will of the Father in all things from the beginning."

To prove that he was truly resurrected, our Lord spoke to the multitude: "Arise and come forth unto me, that ye may thrust your hands into my side, and also that ye may feel the prints of the nails in my hands and in my feet, they ye may know that I am the God of Israel, and the God of the whole earth, and have been slain for the sins of the world."

THE RESURRECTED LORD IN JERUSALEM
(See Matt. 27: 3-5; JST Luke 9: 31; 24: 37-39;
John 20: 24, 26-29)

In conjunction with those events, we turn our attention to the time when the resurrected Savior first appeared in Jerusalem in an upper room to a number of faithful members, including ten of the Twelve Apostles. The reason only ten apostles were present is as follows: (1) Judas Iscariot had committed suicide. (2) For some unexplained reason, Thomas was not present. With the doors closed and locked, "Jesus himself stood in the midst of them." These apostolic witnesses "were terrified and affrighted, and supposed that they had seen a spirit." Jesus spoke these assuring words: "Why are ye troubled? And why do thoughts arise in your hearts? Behold my hands and my feet, that it is I myself: handle me, and see; for a spirit hath not flesh and bones, as ye see me have." A week later, Thomas was present with the ten apostles who had previously seen the risen Lord. Again, the Savior appeared and commanded his doubting apostle to "Reach hither thy finger, and behold my hands; and reach hither thy hand, and thrust it into my side: and be not faithless, but believing." After obeying, Thomas no longer doubted that Jesus was resurrected and had a tangible body of flesh and bones.[8]

The Nephite Multitude Went Forth
(3 Nephi 11: 15-17)

Just as the eleven apostles in Jerusalem complied with the Lord's instruction, so likewise the Nephite "multitude went forth, and thrust their hands into his side, and did feel the prints of the nails in his hands and in his feet; and this they did do, going forth one by one until they had all gone forth, and did see with their eyes and did feel with their hands, and did know of a surety and did bear record, that it was he, of whom it was written by the prophets, that should come."

Mormon testified: "And when they had all gone forth and had witnessed for themselves, they did cry out with one accord, saying: Hosanna! Blessed be the name of the Most High God! And they did fall down at the feet of Jesus [as doubtless we would have done under similar circumstances] and did worship him."

From among this blessed multitude, the resurrected Savior chose twelve men, with Nephi at their head, and to each he gave power to baptize the Nephite people. This Nephi was the son of Nephi, who was the son of Helaman.

Note

1. Dr. Sidney B. Sperry was a Professor of Old Testament Languages and Literature, at Brigham Young University, in Provo, Utah. He is recognized for his literary talents and knowledge of the gospel of Jesus Christ.

2. Bruce R. McConkie was sustained to the First Council of the Seventy, October 6, 1946, at age 31; ordained an apostle, by President

Harold B. Lee, on October 12, 1972, at age 57. He died April 19, 1985, at Salt Lake City, Utah, at age 69.

Elder McConkie was a prolific writer. He is recognized as one of the foremost gospel scholars in the Church. Part of his scholarly works include the following: *Mormon Doctrine, The Doctrinal New Testament Commentary series, The Mortal Messiah: From Bethlehem to Calvary series*; and, the last book written before his death, *A New Witness for the Articles of Faith*.

Chapter Two

The Calling and Ordination
of the Nephite Twelve
(3 Nephi 11: 18-28; Abr. 3: 22-23; 1 Ne. 1: 9-10; 12: 8-10;
Mormon 3: 19; Rev. 21: 10-14; D&C 29: 12)

"This meeting [of the multitude round about the temple, which was in the land Bountiful] must have been called by inspiration," says Dr. Sperry, "probably under Nephi's direction. That it was, is made probable by the fact that all of the Twelve chosen by Jesus were present. None was chosen of those who remained at home."[9]

After the people fell down at the feet of the Savior and worshipped him, our Lord spoke unto "Nephi (for Nephi was among the multitude) and he commanded him that he should come forth." Obediently, this righteous man "arose and went forth, and bowed himself before the Lord and did kiss his feet."

Jesus then asked Nephi to arise. After complying, he received this authoritative instruction: "I give unto you power that ye shall baptize this people when I am again ascended into heaven."

Not only was Nephi given authority to baptize the Nephite people, the Lord "called others"—meaning: eleven other righteous disciples—and "he gave unto them power to baptize."

Concerning those twelve disciples, the Prophet Joseph

Smith[10] has given the following explanation: "This book [meaning: the *Book of Mormon*] also tells us that our Savior made his appearance upon this [the American] continent after His resurrection; that He planted the Gospel here in all its fulness, and richness, and power, and blessing; that they had *Apostles*, Prophets, Pastors, Teachers, and Evangelists . . . "[11] (Italics added)

In addition, Elder Joseph Fielding Smith[12] has written: "While in every instance the Nephite twelve are spoken of as disciples, the fact remains that they had been endowed with divine authority to be special witnesses for Christ among their own people. Therefore, they were virtually apostles to the Nephite race, although their jurisdiction was, as revealed to Nephi, eventually to be subject to the authority and jurisdiction of Peter and the twelve chosen in Palestine."[13]

Concerning the Three Nephites as translated beings, Elder McConkie says: "These three American apostles 'were caught up into heaven, and saw and heard unspeakable things . . . '"[14]

From these statements, we are made aware that the twelve Nephite disciples were actually apostles, with a similar calling as the original Twelve Apostles, who were chosen during the mortal ministry of our Lord.

"It should be pointed out," explains Dr. Sperry, "that although the Nephite Twelve were a quorum of apostles and contemporary with the Twelve in Palestine, they were not *the* Quorum of the Twelve. The Twelve in Palestine must be given that honor . . . . In any question of ultimate authority, however academic, it must be admitted that the Twelve in Palestine had seniority over the Nephite Twelve."[15]

8

In harmony with this statement, President Joseph F. Smith,[16] who was Second Counselor to President John Taylor, said: "It is true the Lord did appoint other Twelve upon this [the American] continent, and His Church flourished and prospered in this land for many years, but the Lord declared that Peter, James and John, and the Twelve that walked with Him at Jerusalem, held the Presidency over them. God may reveal himself to different nations, and establish among them the same Gospel and ordinances as He did anciently, if necessity require, but if these nations should be joined together there would be one head, and all the rest would be subordinate."[17]

From the writings of Moroni—who was the son of Mormon—we find out this information: "Wherefore, I write a few more things, contrary to that which I had supposed; for I had supposed not to have written any more; but I write a few more things, that perhaps they may be of worth unto my brethren, the Lamanites, in some future day, according to the will of the Lord."

Then, this great man revealed this information that was not written previously by his father: "The words of Christ, which he spake unto his disciples, the twelve whom he had chosen, as he laid his hands upon them—And he called them by name [individually], saying: Ye shall call on the Father in my name, in mighty prayer; and after ye have done this ye shall have power that to him upon whom ye shall lay your hands, ye shall give the Holy Ghost; and in my name shall ye give it, for thus do mine apostles.

"Now Christ spake these words unto them at the time of his first appearing; and the multitude heard it not, but the disciples heard it; and on as many as they laid their hands, fell the Holy Ghost" (Moroni 1: 4; 2: 1-3).

Fortunately for us, Mormon wrote the names of the Nephite Twelve: Nephi, Timothy (who is Nephi's brother), "whom [Nephi] had raised from the dead," Jonas (who is a son of Nephi), Mathoni, Mathonihah (who is a brother of Mathoni), Kumen, Kumenonhi, Jeremiah, Shemnon, Jonas, Zedekiah, and Isaiah (3 Ne. 19: 4).

It is worth emphasizing that three members of Nephi's family were called by the resurrected Lord to serve as apostles—himself, a son, and a brother. In addition, two related brothers were also called. This truly verifies that believing blood runs in the veins of righteous families.

Therefore, on the very day that the Savior appeared to the multitude, he called the Nephite Twelve and gave them power and authority to administer the affairs of his Church. However, it is important to point out that long before these apostles were called, the Church of Jesus Christ was already established on the American continent.

THE CHURCH OF JESUS CHRIST
(Mosiah 18: 18; Mosiah 23:16-17)

Many Latter-day Saints have the understanding that Alma, who is the father of Alma, established the Church of Jesus Christ among the Nephite people. To clarify, we turn to Elder Smith for understanding: "While in the wilderness Alma organized his group of believers into a branch of the Church and is spoken of as their founder."[18]

Our apostolic scholar then gives this explanation about Alma: "The main body of the Nephites, under the second King Mosiah, was still intact in the land of Zarahemla. The reference stating that Alma was the founder of their church has reference only to the refugees who were fleeing from the land of the Nephites' first inheritance. In course of time they found their way back to the main body of the Church and Alma was consecrated as the high priest over the Church in all the lands occupied by the Nephites."[19]

As it pertains to the kingdom of God, Elder Smith says: "The colony led by Lehi out of Jerusalem was part of the Church of Jesus Christ. From the day of Adam to the present day, whenever the people obeyed the commandments of the Lord, there was the Church, and people came into it by obeying the same ordinances, which are obeyed today . . . It does not require a complete organization consisting of a branch, ward, and stake to constitute the Church of Jesus Christ. Wherever a person is legally baptized, there is the Church, or by right of that baptism, he becomes a member of it. The kingdom of God and the Church are synonymous terms."[20]

With this information, we again repeat what the resurrected Lord told Nephi: "I give unto you power that ye shall baptize this people when I am again ascended into heaven."

Not only was Nephi given authority to baptize the Nephite people, the Lord "called others"—meaning: eleven other righteous disciples—and "he gave unto them power to baptize."

"It may be asked why Nephi," says Dr. Sperry, "and possibly other members of the Twelve, had to receive authority to baptize (3 Ne. 11: 22), and were themselves required to be baptized, when they had baptized many long years before the Savior's appearance (3 Ne. 7: 23-26).

The answer probably lies in the fact that when our Lord appeared to the Nephites, He proceeded to organize the Church in its fulness, and baptism under the Law of Moses was done away with."[21]

With another view, Elder James E. Talmage[22] says: "We read that before the second appearing of Christ to the Nephites, the chosen twelve were baptized (3 Ne. 19: 10-13). These men had doubtless been baptized before, for Nephi had been empowered not only to baptize but to ordain others to the requisite authority for administering baptism (3 Ne. 7: 23-26). The baptism of the disciples on the morn of the Savior's second visit, was in the nature of a rebaptism, involving a renewal of covenants, and confession of faith in the Lord Jesus."[23]

THE PRIESTHOOD OF THE NEPHITES

Because the Nephite people were living the Law of Moses, it is proper to ask whether they functioned under the Aaronic or the Melchizedek Priesthood? To answer, we again rely upon Elder Smith for knowledge: "The Nephites were descendants of Joseph. Lehi discovered this when reading the brass plates. He was a descendant of Manasseh, and Ishmael, who accompanied him with his family, was of the tribe of Ephraim (Alma 10: 3). Therefore there were no Levites who accompanied Lehi to the Western Hemisphere. Under these conditions the Nephites officiated by virtue of the Melchizedek Priesthood from the days of Lehi to the days of the appearance of our Savior among them."[24]

When the resurrected Savior appeared, he did away

with the Law of Moses and told the multitude: "Marvel not that I said unto you that old things have passed away, and that all things had become new. Behold, I say unto you that the law is fulfilled that was given unto Moses. Behold, I am he that gave the law, and I am he who covenanted with my people Israel; therefore, the law in me is fulfilled, for I have come to fulfil the law; therefore it hath an end" (3 Ne. 15: 3-5).

Now that the Law of Moses was fulfilled, the Nephite Twelve "were receiving a new commission," says Elder McConkie, "as part of a new dispensation . . . Their commission, however, was to administer salvation to the Nephites in the Americas as contrasted with that of the Old World Twelve who were sent to all nations."[25]

Regarding their ordinances in the past, our apostolic scholar states: "They too had been taught true principles and were practicing true ordinances. And yet Jesus now renews and clarifies these policies and procedures among them, as we suppose he did also in Galilee."[26]

NOTE

1. Joseph Smith, Jr. was the first president and prophet of The Church of Jesus Christ of Latter-day Saints. He received the Melchizedek Priesthood, and was ordained an apostle of Jesus Christ, in May 1829, by Peter, James, and John (*See* D&C 20: 2; 27: 12). Though he never served in the Quorum of the Twelve Apostles, the Prophet was the presiding apostle until his death.

At age 24, he was sustained as the First Elder of the Church on April 6, 1830; ordained a high priest on June 3, 1831; at age 26, he was sustained as President of the High Priesthood on January 25, 1832; at age 38, he was martyred at Carthage Jail, in Carthage, Illinois.

2. Joseph Fielding Smith was ordained an apostle on April 7, 1910, by President Joseph F. Smith, at age 33; sustained as Acting President of the Quorum of the Twelve Apostles on September 30, 1950; sustained as the President of the Quorum of the Twelve Apostles on April 9, 1951; sustained as Counselor in the First Presidency on October 29, 1965; ordained and set apart as the President of the Church on January 23, 1970, at age 93; he died July 2, 1972, in Salt Lake City, Utah, at age 95.

3. Joseph F. Smith was ordained an apostle and named as a Counselor to the First Presidency on July 1, 1866, by President Brigham Young, at age 27; set apart as a member of the Quorum of the Twelve Apostles on October 8, 1867; released as a Counselor to the First Presidency at the death of President Young on August 29, 1877; sustained as Second Counselor to President John Taylor on October 10, 1880; released at the death of President Taylor on July 25, 1887; sustained as Second Counselor to President Wilford Woodruff on April 7, 1889; sustained as Second Counselor to President Lorenzo Snow on September 13, 1898; sustained as First Counselor to President Snow on October 6, 1901, not set apart to this position; released at the death of President Snow on October 10, 1901; ordained and set apart as the President of the Church on October 17, 1901, at age 62; he died November 19, 1918, at Salt Lake City, Utah, at age 80.

4. James E. Talmage was ordained an apostle on December 8, 1911, by President Joseph F. Smith, at age 49. He died at Salt Lake City, Utah on July 27, 1933, at age 70. Among his scholarly works, he is most recognized for writing *Jesus the Christ*, a book that is endorsed and published by The Church of Jesus Christ of Latter-day Saints. He is also the author of *The Articles of Faith*.

Chapter Three

The Role of the Nephite Twelve in Christ's Church

(1 Cor. 12: 28; Eph. 4: 11-15;Abr. 3: 22-23; 1 Ne. 1: 9-10; 12: 8-10; Mormon 3: 19;Rev. 21: 10-14; D&C 29: 12)

To help people identify the true church of Christ, Paul, who was an Old World apostle, has written the following information: "And God hath set some in the church, *first apostles*, secondarily prophets, thirdly teachers." Then, the following are given to bless and strengthen the organization: "after that miracles, then gifts of healings, helps, governments, diversities of tongues" (Italics added).[27]

To make clear why our Lord established his Church—both in the Old World and in America—with various officers in the organization, we rely again upon Paul for understanding: "And he gave some, apostles; and some, prophets; and some evangelists; and some, pastors and teachers; For the perfecting of the saints, for the work of the ministry, for the edifying of the body of Christ: Till we all come in the unity of the faith, and of the knowledge of the Son of God, unto a perfect man, unto the measure of the stature of the fulness of Christ. That we henceforth be no more children, tossed to and fro, and carried about with every wind of doctrine, by the sleight of men, and cunning craftiness, whereby they lie in wait to deceive."

Therefore, the true Church of Jesus Christ will have

apostles, prophets, and teachers, all of whom are called of God and endowed with power to "regulate all the affairs of the same in all nations." And where none of these officers are found in the Church, the Kingdom of God is not established on the earth. Therefore, these servants "speaking the truth in love," guide and direct the Lord's Church on earth.

Among the "noble and great ones," as seen by Abraham, the Twelve Apostles—no matter what dispensation of time is involved—were chosen, before they were born, to be rulers in Christ's Church. They were foreordained to come and serve as special witnesses of our Lord and Savior.

Six hundred years before the birth of Christ, Lehi saw the Jewish Twelve Apostles in vision. Nephi, who was the son of Lehi, wrote these informative words: "And it came to pass that he saw One descending out of the midst of heaven, and he beheld that his luster was above that of the sun at noon-day. And he also saw twelve others following him, and their brightness did exceed that of the stars in the firmament."

When the Nephite Twelve were chosen, our Lord gave them the same authority as he had given the Jewish Twelve. From Nephi and Mormon, we read the following information about the two sets of Twelve Apostles: "And I write also unto the remnant of this people, who shall also be judged by the twelve whom Jesus chose in this land; and they shall be judged by the other twelve whom Jesus chose in the land of Jerusalem. And these things doth the Spirit manifest unto me; therefore I write unto you all."

By reason that there are twelve tribes in Israel, so there are Twelve Apostles who preside over Israel and the world. In its celestial glory, John the Revelator saw Jerusalem "descending out of heaven from God." This city "had a wall great and high, and [it] had twelve gates," and on these gates, "are the names of the twelve tribes of the children of Israel" And, "the wall of the city had twelve foundations, and [on] them [were written] the names of the twelve apostles of the Lamb."

Therefore, John the Revelator saw the Jewish Twelve, who will preside over the Nephite Twelve, as well as Latter-day Twelve, in our dispensation. Excepting Judas Iscariot—who betrayed our Lord in Jerusalem—all who are called to serve in the Quorum of the Twelve Apostles "are righteous forever; for because of their faith in the Lamb of God their garments are made white in his blood."

In addition, the Lord has revealed the following information about the second coming of Christ: "And again, verily, verily, I say unto you, and it hath gone forth in a firm decree, by the will of the Father, that mine apostles, the Twelve, which were with me in my ministry at Jerusalem, shall stand at my right hand at the day of my coming in a pillar of fire, being clothed with robes of righteousness, with crowns upon their heads, in glory even as I am, to judge the whole house of Israel, even as many as have loved me and kept my commandments, and none else."

From ancient times until the present, the members of the First Presidency and the Quorum of the Twelve are called and sustained as prophets, seers, and revelators. With a similar calling as the Twelve Apostles in Jerusalem, the Nephite Twelve were also designated as prophets, seers, and revelators for the Nephite people. Therefore, let us find out about these sacred titles.[28]

APOSTLES
(Heb. 3:1; D&C 107: 23, 33)

Because the Nephite Twelve were called by our Lord to be apostles, let us find out the meaning of the word *apostle*. Elder Talmage says, "The word 'apostle' is an Anglicized form derived from the Greek *apostolos*, meaning literally 'one who is sent,' and connoting an envoy or official messenger, who speaks and acts by the authority of one superior to himself. In this sense Paul afterward applied the title to Christ as one specially sent and commissioned of the Father."[29]

From Elder McConkie, we learn the significance of this holy calling: "This is the supreme office in the church in all dispensations because those so ordained hold both the fulness of the priesthood and all of the keys of the kingdom of God on earth. The President of the Church serves in that high and exalted position because he is the senior apostle of God on earth and thus can direct the manner in which all other apostles and priesthood holders use their priesthood."[30]

Considering those individuals who are called to be apostles, we rely once more upon Elder McConkie for information: "An apostle is an ordained office in the Melchizedek Priesthood, and those so ordained . . . are set apart as members of the Quorum of the Twelve and are given the keys and power to preside over the church and kingdom and regulate all of the affairs of God on earth."[31]

In harmony with what Elder Talmage wrote—that an apostle is "one who is sent," Elder McConkie explains, quoting: "Apostles are 'special witnesses of the name of Christ in all the world.' They are also 'a Traveling Presiding High Council, to officiate in the name of the Lord, under the direction of the Presidency of the Church, agreeable to the institution of heaven; to build up the church, and regulate all the affairs of the same in all nations, first unto the Gentiles and secondly unto the Jews.'"[32]

Therefore, each of the Nephite Twelve—just like those who are called to be apostles in our dispensation—were to be a "special witness of the name of Christ" and was to "build up the church, and regulate all the affairs of the same . . ." upon the American continent.

PROPHETS
(Numbers 11: 29; Rev. 19: 10)

Concerning prophets, we rely once again upon Elder McConkie for information: "Next to apostles come prophets. They are persons who have 'the testimony of Jesus,' which 'is the spirit of prophecy' . . . . The prophetic position is not an ordained office in the priesthood, although every person who holds the priesthood is or should be a prophet . . . . The First Presidency and the Twelve are sustained as prophets, seers, and revelators to the church. The President is the presiding prophet on earth and as such is the one through whom revelation is sent forth to the world and for the guidance of the whole body of believing saints."[33]

SEERS
(Mosiah 8: 13-18; Matt. 16: 18)

"Seers," explains Elder McConkie, "are specially selected prophets who are authorized to use the Urim and Thummim and who are empowered to know past, present, and future things. 'A gift which is greater can no man have.'"[34]

REVELATORS
(D&C 77:2: 100: 11; 128: 6; D&C 107: 92; 124: 94, 125)

Again, Elder McConkie provides this information: "Anyone who receives revelation from the Lord and conveys the revealed truth to another is a *revelator*. Joseph Smith was a revelator to Sidney Rigdon; the beloved disciple, because of the great revelations he left for the world, is known as John the Revelator. The President of the Church is a revelator for the Church, as also are the members of the First Presidency, [and] the Council of the Twelve . . . "[35]

We have no knowledge whether any members of Nephite Twelve served in the First Presidency, or that the senior apostle became the president of Christ's Church in the Americas. The only information we have is that Christ chose twelve men, with Nephi at their head, to be his apostles. Each had been endowed with divine authority to be special witnesses for Christ. By virtue that they were called to be apostles, they were designated as prophets, seers, and revelators for the Nephite people.

Chapter Four

Baptism of the Nephite Twelve
(3 Nephi 11: 23-41)

Directing his remarks to the Nephite Twelve, our Lord gave these important instructions: "Verily I say unto you, that whoso repenteth of his sins through your words, and desireth to be baptized in my name, on this wise shall ye baptize them—Behold, ye shall go down and stand in the water, and in my name shall ye baptize them." Jesus then gave them the fixed prayer they should use, which is very similar to the one that has been given in this dispensation (D&C 20: 73). Said he: "And now behold, these are the words which ye shall say, calling them by name, saying: 'Having authority given me of Jesus Christ, I baptize you in the name of the Father, and of the Son, and of the Holy Ghost. Amen.'"

After giving the prayer, our Lord instructed that the apostles should "immerse [those to be baptized] in the water, and [afterwards they] should come forth again out of the water."

The Baptism of Jesus
(Matt. 3: 13-17; JST Matt. 3: 42-46; Mark 1: 9-11)

In conjunction with this instruction, we turn to the account of the baptism of our Lord, in the Old World:

From the Joseph Smith Translation of Matthew, we find this information: Approaching John the Baptist, Jesus asked to be baptized. "But John refused him, saying, I have need to be baptized of thee, and why comest thou to me? And Jesus, answering said unto him, Suffer me to be baptized of thee, for thus it becometh us to fulfil all righteousness. Then he suffered him (meaning: John agreed to baptize Jesus). And John went down into the water [with our Lord] and baptized him. And Jesus when he was baptized, went up straightway out of the water . . ."

Marks versions reads: "And straightway [Jesus] coming up out of the water . . ."

Just as the resurrected Lord had instructed the Nephite Apostles in the proper ordinance of baptism, John the Baptist baptized Jesus with the identical ordinance. Thus, the individual being baptized was to be immersed in water, by the one performing the baptism. After immersion, the one performing the baptism was to help the baptized individual to come up out of the water.

Returning again to the account in Third Nephi, we find out that after Jesus spoke of the oneness of the members of the Godhead, he stated: "And according as I have commanded you thus shall ye baptize. And there shall be no disputations among you, as there have hitherto been; neither shall there be disputations among you concerning the points of my doctrine, as there have hitherto been" (3 Ne. 11: 27-28).

"The Master then emphasized to the Twelve," explains Dr. Sperry, "the basic principles of repentance and baptism. He who would surrender himself to those principles was to be visited with fire and the Holy Ghost, which bears record of the Father and the Son. Unless they repented and became as little children, and were baptized, they could in no wise inherit the kingdom of God. Anyone who built upon any other doctrine would find himself upon a sandy foundation, and the gates of hell would stand open to receive him."[36]

Without giving a thorough account of the teachings and events that transpired during the Savior's first day visit, we turn our attention to the baptism of the Twelve the following day.

THE NEPHITE TWELVE WERE BAPTIZED
(3 Nephi 19: 1-14)

The first appearance of Jesus had been "noised abroad" that night, and on the second day an even greater number of people gathered to behold and listen to the Savior. Because the "multitude was so great," the Twelve "did cause that they should be separated into twelve bodies."

In addition, the apostles had the multitude kneel and pray unto the Father in the name of Jesus. The members of the Twelve also prayed, especially that "the Holy Ghost should be given unto them." At the conclusion of this prayer service, the apostles proceeded to the water's edge, "and the multitude followed them."

Here "Nephi went down into the water and was baptized." We have no knowledge of the individual who performed this ordinance for this righteous man. From the explicit instructions given previously by our Lord, we are not justified in thinking that Nephi baptized himself.

Afterward, he performed this same ordinance for the other members of the Twelve; for as the record states: "And he baptized all those whom Jesus had chosen."

Following the baptism of the apostles, "they were filled with the Holy Ghost and with fire." Concerning the phrase, "with fire," Mormon provides this information: "And behold, they were encircled about as if it were by fire; and it came down from heaven, and the multitude did witness it, and did bear record." Not only did this fiery manifestation occur, "angels did come down out of heaven and did minister unto them." Then, "while the angels were ministering unto the disciples, behold, Jesus came and stood in the midst and ministered unto them."

Mormon wrote that after Jesus "had ascended into heaven—the second time that he showed himself unto" the multitude, "the disciples whom Jesus had chosen began from that time forth to baptize and to teach as many as did come unto them." Considering those individuals who were baptized by the Twelve, this great historian says, "and as many as were baptized in the name of Jesus were filled with the Holy Ghost." In conclusion, he wrote these explanatory words: "And they who were baptized in the name of Jesus were called the church of Christ" (3 Ne. 26: 15, 17, 21).

Chapter Five

THE DESIRES OF THE NEPHITE TWELVE
(3 Nephi 28)

During his three-day ministry on the American continent, Jesus also instituted the sacrament, spoke a marvelous prayer, and gave inspiring instructions and teachings. He "healed all their sick, and their lame, and opened the eyes of their blind and unstopped the ears of the deaf, and even had done all manner of cures among them, and raised a man from the dead, and had shown forth his power unto them . . ." (3 Ne. 26: 15). Children and "babes did open their mouths and utter marvelous things; and the things which they did utter were forbidden that there should not any man write them" (3 Ne. 26: 16).

To repeat: After the Twelve were baptized, they were filled with the Holy Ghost and were encircled about with fire. Angels also came down from heaven and ministered unto them (3 Ne. 19: 10-14).

From all that had transpired during this glorious three-day ministry of the resurrected Savior, we are safe in believing that the Nephite Twelve were highly enthused spiritually. We now turn our attention to the time when the Savior asked each apostle this searching question: "What is it that ye desire of me, after that I am gone to the Father?"

Nine answered Jesus: "We desire that after we have

lived unto the age of man, that our ministry, wherein thou has called us, may have an end, that we may speedily come unto thee in thy kingdom."

This rewarding answer was spoken by the Lord: "Blessed are ye because ye desired this thing of me; therefore, after that ye are seventy and two years old ye shall come unto me in my kingdom; and with me ye shall find rest."

We have no knowledge whether those nine apostles died on the day they turned seventy-two, or sometime during that year. No matter when that event happened, we can be assured that they received the desired blessing from the Lord.

THE THREE NEPHITES REMAINED SILENT
(3 Nephi 28: 4-7)

Jesus then "turned himself unto the three, and said unto them: What will ye that I should do unto you, when I am gone unto the Father?" Mormon then reveals this insightful information: "And they sorrowed in their hearts, for they durst not speak unto him the thing which they desired." Accordingly, would we be amiss in thinking that because these three were very humble and very respectful, they did not want to verbally ask the Lord—with the other nine apostles listening—to live upon the earth until his Second Coming?

"Behold, I know your thoughts," said Jesus, "and ye have desired the thing which John, my beloved, who was with me in my ministry, before that I was lifted up by the Jews, desired of me."

Our Savior then declared: "Therefore, more blessed are ye [than the other nine apostles] for ye shall never taste of death; but ye shall live to behold all the doings of the Father unto the children of men, even until all things shall be fulfilled according to the will of the Father, when I shall come in my glory with the powers of heaven."

From these expressions, it is proper to wonder what type of lives those three were to have. To assist us, we use the well-chosen words of Elder McConkie: "Eternal life—no, not that glorious immortality in which resurrected beings become like their God, but to live forever on earth, as mortals, without disease or sorrow, having health and vigor, preaching the gospel and being witnesses to and participants in all that was to be!"[37] Thereby, we gain a better understanding of the marvelous gift that was given those three American apostles.

PETER WAS TOLD OF JOHN'S TRANSLATION
(John 21: 18-25)

Considering the Lord's comment that the three had "desired the thing which John, my beloved . . . desired of me," we turn our attention to a conversation about John, that was spoken in the Old World.[38] As our Lord and the senior apostle walked together, Peter, "turning about," saw John—curious as to what would happen to his close colleague and friend—and asked: "Lord, and what shall this man do?"

Jesus answered, "If I will that he tarry till I come, what is that to thee?" He further told Peter: "Follow thou me." The beloved apostle also wrote: "Then went this saying abroad among the brethren, that [John] should not die."

John's own account of his translation was revealed to the Prophet Joseph Smith. As it pertains to our Savior's words to the senior apostle, we read:

> And for this cause the Lord said unto Peter: If I will that he tarry till I come, what is that to thee? For he desired of me that he might bring souls unto me, but thou desiredst that thou mightest speedily come unto me in my kingdom. I say unto thee, Peter, this was a good desire; but my beloved has desired that he might do more, or a greater work yet among men than what he has before done. Yea, he [John] has undertaken a greater work; therefore I will make him as flaming fire and a ministering angel; he shall minister for those who shall be heirs of salvation who dwell on the earth. And I will make thee [Peter] to minister for him [John] and for [his] brother James; and unto you three I will give this power and the keys of this ministry until I come. Verily I say unto you [Peter], ye shall both [Peter and John] have according to your desires, for ye both joy in that which ye have desired" (D&C 7: 4-8).

"That John still lives in the embodied state," says Elder Talmage, "and shall remain in the flesh until the Lord's yet future advent, is attested by later revelation. In company with his martyred and resurrected companions, Peter and James, and the 'disciple whom Jesus loved' has officiated in the restoration of the Holy Apostleship in this the dispensation of the fulness of times."[39]

"Never Endure the Pains of Death"
(3 Nephi 28: 8)

Returning again to the account in Third Nephi, we learn what the Savior told those three apostles: "And ye shall never endure the pains of death; but when I shall come in my glory ye shall be changed in the twinkling of an eye from mortality to immortality; and then shall ye be blessed in the kingdom of my Father."

From these expressions, we find out that those three would never experience death as we know it, but they would be changed "in the twinkling of an eye from mortality to immortality." Elder McConkie says:

> As a matter of doctrine, death is universal; every mortal thing, whether plant or animal or man, shall surely die. Jacob said: 'Death hath passed upon all men, to fulfil the merciful plan of the great Creator' (2 Ne. 9: 6). There are no exceptions, not even among translated beings. Paul said: 'As in Adam all die, even so in Christ shall all be made alive' (1 Cor. 15: 22). Again the dominion of death over all is acclaimed. But the Lord says of all his saints, not that they will not die, but that 'those that die in me shall not taste of death, for it shall be sweet unto them; And they that die not in me, wo unto them, for their death is bitter' (D&C 42: 46-47). The distinction is between dying as such and tasting of death itself. Again the Lord says: 'He that liveth when the Lord shall come, and hath kept the faith, blessed is he; nevertheless, it is appointed to him to die at the age of man. Wherefore, children shall grow up until they become old; old men shall die; but they shall not sleep in the dust, but they shall be changed in the twinkling of an eye' (D&C 63: 50-51). Thus, this change from mortality to immortality,

though almost instantaneous, is both a death and a resurrection.[40]

Concluding his remarks about translated beings, our apostolic scholar says:

> *Thus, translated beings do not suffer death as we normally define it, meaning the separation of body and spirit; nor do they receive a resurrection as we ordinarily describe it, meaning that the body rises from the dust and the spirit enters again into its fleshly home. But they do pass through death and are changed from mortality to immortality, in the eternal sense, and they thus both die and are resurrected in the eternal sense. This, we might add, is why Paul wrote: Behold, I shew you a mystery; We shall not all sleep, but we shall all be changed, In a moment, in the twinkling of an eye, at the last trump; for the trumpet shall sound, and the dead shall be raised incorruptible, and we shall be changed (1 Cor. 15: 51-52).*[41]

In harmony with these comments, President Heber C. Kimball,[42] First Counselor to President Brigham Young states: "We read of men who have been translated, but they must pass through a change which is equal to death, for it is appointed that all men shall die . . ."[43] Likewise, Elder Wilford Woodruff[44] declared: " The whole human family, heathen, pagan, Christian and Jew, know that this is not their home [earth], and that all have got to die, they cannot escape the law of death; even if translated, as some were anciently, they have to undergo a change equivalent to death."[45]

THEIR GREAT DESIRES, FAITH AND REWARDS
(3 Nephi 28: 9-11)

As to the blessings and rewards of the three, we continue with the Lord's words: "And again, ye shall not have pain while ye shall dwell in the flesh, neither sorrow save it be for the sins of the world; and all this will I do because of the thing which ye have desired of me, for ye have desired that ye might bring the souls of men unto me, while the world shall stand."

By reason that these special men will never suffer the ailments of mortality, they will never experience physical pain. Because they will never experience pain, or suffer death as we normally define it, they will never have sorrow, excepting for the sins of the world.

Concerning missionary work in general, the Prophet Joseph Smith received this instruction: "Therefore, if ye have desires to serve God ye are called to the work" (D&C 4: 3). Due to their great *desires* of bringing souls unto Christ, those three Nephite apostles were called to this important work, by becoming translated beings.

Besides their great desires of bring souls unto Christ, we learn of another reason why they became translated beings. Elder McConkie has aptly written: "As his crowning illustration of faith among mortals, Moroni names the translation of the Three Nephites. 'And it was by faith that the three disciples obtained a promise that they should not taste of death,' he says, 'and they obtained not the promise until after their faith.' What greater miracle could there be among us mortals than the miracle of translation? What power but the power of God can extend the life of mortal man on earth for thousands of added years? And what power does Deity possess except the power of faith?"[46] (Ether 12: 17)

In his last recorded words to the three, our Lord gave this glorious promise: "And for this cause ye shall have fulness of joy; and ye shall sit down in the kingdom of my Father; yea, your joy shall be full, even as the Father hath given me fulness of joy; and ye shall be even as I am, and I am even as the Father; and the Father and I are one; And the Holy Ghost beareth record of the Father and me; and the Father giveth the Holy Ghost unto the children of men, because of me."

NOTE

1. Heber C. Kimball was ordained an apostle on February 14, 1835, under the hands of Oliver Cowdery, David Whitmer, and Martin Harris, at age 33; sustained as First Counselor to President Brigham Young on December 27, 1847, at age 46; died on June 22, 1868, at Salt Lake City, Utah, at age 67.

2. Wilford Woodruff was ordained an apostle on April 26, 1839, by President Brigham Young, at age 32; sustained as the President of the Quorum of the Twelve Apostles on October 10, 1880; sustained as the President of the Church on April 7, 1889, at age 82; died on September 2, 1898, at age 91.

Chapter Six

THE TRANSFIGURATION
AND MINISTRY OF THE THREE NEPHITES
(3 Nephi 28: 12-40)

Because the Book of Mormon is an abridgement of sacred writings, we are most thankful that Mormon made space on the plates to write of events that transpired in the lives of the Three Nephites as translated beings. From his writings, we find out that after Jesus had spoken those wondrous words, he touched the nine apostles with his finger, but not "the three who were to tarry." Then, our Lord departed.

"And behold, the heavens were opened, and they [those three] were caught up into heaven, and saw and heard unspeakable things. And it was forbidden them that they should utter; neither was it given unto them power that they could utter the things which they saw and heard; And whether they were in the body or out of the body, they could not tell; for it did seem unto them like a transfiguration of them, that they were changed from this body of flesh into an immortal state, that they could behold the things of God."

"Transfiguration," explains Elder McConkie, "is a special change in appearance and nature which is wrought upon a person or thing by the power of God. This divine transformation is from a lower to a higher state; it results in a more exalted, impressive, and glorious condition."[47] Accordingly, this special change occurred with the bodies of the Three Nephites, in order that individually and collectively, they "could behold the things of God."

> *It was with them as with Paul and Joseph Smith and others of the prophets. There are no words that can convey the spiritual feelings or the truths learned by those who receive these greater manifestations of divine understanding. Speaking of himself, Paul says he was 'caught up to the third heaven,' which is the celestial kingdom—'whether in the body, or out of the body, I cannot tell: God knoweth,' he says—and that he 'heard unspeakable words, which it is not lawful for a man to utter' (2 Cor. 12: 1-4). After recording the vision of the degrees of glory, Joseph Smith spoke similarly of other things that he had seen and heard while enwrapped in the heavenly manifestation then vouchsafed to him (D&C 76: 114-119 and D&C 137: 1).* —Elder Bruce R. McConkie[48]

THEIR ENDOWMENTS

As to what happened when those three apostles "were caught up into heaven," Elder Franklin D. Richards[49] expressed these thought-provoking comments: "They wanted to tarry until Jesus came, and that they might, He took them into the heavens and endowed them with the power of translation, probably in one of Enoch's temples, and brought them back to the earth. Thus they received power to live until the coming of the Son of Man. I believe He took them to Enoch's city and gave them their endowments there."[50]

For additional understanding—and with the full realization that from the days of Adam to our day, the ordinance of the endowment is performed in sacred places upon this earth, for both the living and the dead—we read what President Wilford Woodruff said, as printed in a publication, *Deseret News Weekly*: "Bro. W. Woodruff related an instance of the appearance of one of the three Nephites, testified that Joseph Smith gave him his endowments . . ."[51]

Other than Elder Richards comments, we have no knowledge of what happened when those special men were caught up into heaven. The same applies to President Woodruff's remarks concerning one of the Three Nephites receiving his endowments from the Prophet Joseph Smith.

It is important to point out that President Wilford Woodruff kept detailed *Journals*, "through sixty-three eventful years," and most of the early history of the Church is obtained from his daily journals.[52]

"A CHANGE WROUGHT UPON THEIR BODIES"
(3 Nephi 28: 37-40; 4 Nephi 1: 14, 29-33)

Considering the change that came upon the Three Nephites, Mormon received this information: "But behold, since I wrote, I have inquired of the Lord, and he hath made it manifest unto me that there must needs be a change wrought upon their bodies, or else it needs be that they must taste of death; Therefore, that they might not taste of death there was a change wrought upon their bodies [meaning: they became translated beings], that they might not suffer pain nor sorrow save it were for the sins of the world."

In addition, this great historian was given this knowledge: "Now this change was not equal to that which shall take place at the last day [meaning: being resurrected]; but there was a change wrought upon them, insomuch that Satan could have no power over them, that he could not tempt them; and they were sanctified [meaning: they were clean, pure, and spotless from sin] in the flesh, that they were holy, and that the powers of the earth could not hold them."

Mormon was then informed of their great reward: "And in this state [as translated beings] they were to remain until the judgment day of Christ; and at that day they were to receive a greater change [meaning: to physically die and receive a full resurrection, wherein the spirit and body are forever united], and to be received into the kingdom of the Father to go no more out [meaning, they will enter the highest degree of the celestial kingdom], but to dwell with God eternally in the heavens [meaning: each will become like the Father, by becoming a God].

After returning from heaven, as the record states, the three "did again minister upon the face of the earth; nevertheless they did not minister of the things which they had heard and seen, because of the commandment which was given them in heaven." Therefore, those special apostles only taught the Nephite people the saving truths of the gospel of Jesus Christ, which gospel is the same that was revealed to the Prophet Joseph Smith in our dispensation.

"Though they lived and labored as men among their fellows," Elder Talmage has written, "preaching, baptizing, and conferring the Holy Ghost upon all who gave heed to their words, the enemies to the truth were powerless to do them injury. Somewhat later than a hundred and seventy years after the Lord's last visitation, malignant persecution was waged against the Three."[53]

Mormon says:

"And they were cast into prison by them who did not belong to the church." By their command, the "prisons could not hold them, for they were rent in twain." They were cast into pits of the earth, but they "did smite the earth with the word of God, insomuch that by his power they were delivered out of the depths of the earth; and therefore they could not dig pits sufficient to hold them."

"And thrice they were cast into a furnace and received no harm." In addition, they were cast twice "into a den of wild beasts; and behold they did play with the beasts as a child with a suckling lamb, and received no harm."

Names of the Three Nephites
(3 Nephi 28: 23-25)

After those events happened, the record states that the three apostles went "forth among all the people of Nephi, and did preach the gospel of Jesus Christ unto all people upon the face of the land . . ."

Then, these revealing words are written: "And now I, Mormon, make an end of speaking concerning these things for a time. Behold, I was about to write the names of those who were never to taste of death, but the Lord forbade; therefore I write them not, for they are hid from the world."

We now advance to the time of the early history of the Church, in our dispensation. On Monday, April 10, 1843, a special conference was held for the purpose of ordaining Elders and sending them forth to build up the Church. One of those men was Oliver B. Huntington.[54]

From his personal history, which is housed in a special collections library at Brigham Young University, in Provo, Utah, we read from page 43 this entry: "February 16, 1895: I am willing to state that the names of the 3 Nephites who do not sleep in the earth are *Jeremiah*, *Zedekiah*, and *Kumenonhi*." (Italics added)

Though this information is highly interesting, it is important to point out that no other reference can substantiate his journal entry. Therefore, the reader will have to determine whether Brother Huntington's comments are only conjecture, or inspired words of truth.

Returning again to the ministry of the Three Nephites, as recorded by Mormon, we find out that about A.D. 322, "wickedness did prevail upon the face of the whole land, insomuch that the Lord did take away his beloved disciples, and the work of miracles and of healing did cease because of the iniquity of the people" (Mormon 1: 13). Then, in the year A.D. 401, Moroni—who is the son of Mormon—wrote these words: "And there are none that do know the true God save it be the disciples of Jesus, who did tarry in the land until the wickedness of the people was so great that the Lord would not suffer them to remain with the people; and whether they be upon the face of the land no man knoweth. But Behold, my father and I have seen them, and they have ministered unto us" (Mormon 8: 10-11; See also 3 Nephi 28: 26).

As to their continuing mortal ministry, we know only that they shall be among the Jews, and among the

Gentiles, and among 'all the scattered tribes of Israel,' and among 'all nations, kindreds, tongues and people, and shall bring out of them unto Jesus many souls.' And this also applies to John the Beloved. 'And they are as the angels of God, and if they shall pray unto the Father in the name of Jesus they can show themselves unto whatsoever man it seemeth them good. Therefore, great and marvelous works shall be wrought by them, before the great and coming day when all people must surely stand before the judgment-seat of Christ; Yea even among the Gentiles shall there be a great and marvelous work wrought by them, before the judgment day (3 Nephi 28: 27-32). —Elder Bruce R. McConkie[55]

NOTE

1. Franklin Dewy Richards was ordained an apostle on February 12, 1849, by Heber C. Kimball, at age 27; sustained as President of the Quorum of the Twelve Apostles on September 13, 1898; he died December 9, 1899, at age 78.

Chapter Seven

THE DOCTRINE OF TRANSLATION

To better understand the special powers and abilities of the Three Nephites, we turn to the Prophet Joseph Smith for knowledge concerning translated beings. Said he: "Now the doctrine of translation is a power which belongs to this [the Melchizedek] Priesthood."[56]

Using a definition, we learn that priesthood is the power and authority of God delegated to man on earth to act in all things for the salvation of men. Therefore, by the power of the priesthood—which is the power of God—the Three Nephites became translated beings, to act in all things for the salvation of men.

The Prophet further stated: "Many have supposed that the doctrine of translation was a doctrine whereby men were taken immediately into the presence of God, and into an eternal fulness, but this is a mistaken idea, Their place of habitation is that of the terrestrial order . . ."[57]

While residing upon this earth, their place of habitation is that of the terrestrial order (3 Ne. 28: 8). When they are finally changed in the twinkling of an eye from mortality to immortality, their place of habitation will be of the celestial order (3 Ne. 28: 10, 40).

To support the statement that the Three Nephites still reside upon this earth, Elder Wilford Woodruff stated:

"The first quorum of Apostles [who were with Jesus in Jerusalem] were all put to death, except John [the Revelator], and we are informed that he still remains on the earth, though his body has doubtless undergone some change. Three of the Nephites, chosen here [in America] by the Lord Jesus as his Apostles, had the same promise— that they should not taste death until Christ came, and *they still remain on the earth in the flesh.*"[58] (Italics added)

With this information, we continue with the Prophet Joseph Smith's words: "He [Our Lord] held in reserve [translated beings] to be ministering angels unto many planets, and who as yet have not entered into so great a fulness as those who are resurrected from the dead.

"Translation obtains deliverance from the tortures and sufferings of the body, but their existence will prolong as to the labors and toils of the ministry, before they can enter into so great a rest and glory."[59]

These comments by the Prophet support and confirm the words of Mormon concerning the Three Nephites, "that there must needs be a change wrought upon their bodies, or else it needs be that they must taste of death." In addition, that "this change was not equal to that which shall take place at the last day" (3 Ne. 28: 37-39).

In harmony with these statements, Elder Orson Pratt[60] spoke about the inhabitants of the city of Enoch, who were translated and taken from this earth: ". . . *they learned the great doctrine and principle of translation*, for that is a doctrine the same as the doctrine of the resurrection of the dead, which is among the first principles of the plan of salvation; and we may also say that the doctrine of translation, which is intimately connected with that of the resurrection, is also one of the first principles of the doctrine of Christ."[61] (Italics added)

"A CHANGE WROUGHT UPON THEIR BODIES"
(3 Nephi 28: 15, 37-40)

In order that the Three Nephites "might not taste of death there was a change wrought upon their bodies," wrote Mormon. What then caused this special *change*? Likewise, what is "the great doctrine and principle of translation," spoken by Elder Pratt? To help answer these intriguing questions, we rely upon the knowledge of three General Authorities. Elder McConkie wrote: "Some mortals have been translated. In this state, they are not subject to sorrow or to disease or to death. *No longer does blood (the life-giving element of our present mortality) flow in their veins. Procreation ceases.* If they then had children, their offspring would be denied a mortal probation, which all worthy spirits must receive in due course. They have power to move and live in both a mortal and an unseen sphere. All translated beings undergo another change in their bodies when they gain full immortality. This change is the equivalent of a resurrection. All mortals, after death, are also resurrected."[62] (Italics added)

It is important to emphasize that translated beings undergo one additional *change* in their bodies (refer to number 3), which is not common with the rest of mankind: (1) Through the birth process—which is universal with all people who live upon this earth—they became mortal. (2) Then, by the power of the Melchizedek

Priesthood—which is the power of God—they became translated beings. From Elder McConkie, we find out that blood no longer flows in their veins. Also, that procreation ceases. *This change is not universal with all mankind.* (3) When translated beings are finally "changed in the twinkling of an eye from mortality to immortality," they receive a resurrected body. The resurrection is universal with all people who live upon this earth.

Concerning our resurrected Lord, President Brigham Young[63] declared: "The blood he [Jesus Christ] spilled upon Mount Calvary, he did not receive again into his veins. That was poured out, and when he was resurrected, *another element took the place of the blood.* It will be so with every person who receives a resurrection: the blood will not be resurrected with the body, being designed only to sustain the life of the present organization."[64]

What then is the element that takes the place of blood? To answer, we rely upon the wisdom of Brother Charles W. Penrose:[65] "The corruptible blood was purged from the veins [of Jesus Christ], *and incorruptible spiritual fluid occupied its place.* It was buried a natural body, it was resurrected a spiritual body."[66] (Italics added)

Regarding translated beings, we repeat what Elder McConkie says: "No longer does blood (the life-giving element of our present mortality) flow in their veins."[67]

As *blood* does not flow in the veins of translated and resurrected beings, but *incorruptible spiritual fluid*, it is natural to ask: What then determines the difference between them? With interest, we discover that Mormon provided the answer. Said he about the Three Nephites: "Now this change [in their bodies] was not equal to that which shall take place at the last day . . . And in this state they were to remain until the judgment day of Christ; and at that day they were to receive a greater change . . ." (3 Ne. 28: 39-40). From these teachings, it appears evident that there are two types of incorruptible spiritual fluid. One type changed the Three Nephites into translated beings, "which is not equal to that which shall take place at the last day." When they are finally changed, "in the twinkling of an eye from mortality to immortality," the other type will turn them into resurrected beings, whereby they "receive a greater change" (3 Ne. 28: 8). Accordingly, the corruptible blood was purged from the veins of those three Nephite apostles, and incorruptible spiritual fluid occupied its place. Thus, this glorious element caused the *change* to come upon their bodies, "in order that they might not taste of death," as spoken by Mormon. With this knowledge, we have a better understanding of "the great doctrine and principle of translation," as spoken by Elder Pratt.

POWERS AND ABILITIES OF THE THREE NEPHITES

Because the Three Nephites had this special change come upon their bodies, "they can show themselves unto whatsoever man it seemeth them good" (3 Ne. 28: 30). As President Anthony W. Ivins,[68] Second Counselor to President Heber J. Grant, stated: ". . . in other words, they were not visible to whomsoever they made themselves not visible."[69]

Then, Elder Melvin J. Ballard[70] revealed the following information: "Although they had the ability to live in the earth among men," they had power over the elements of earth, power over the law of gravitation, *by which they could move over the face of the earth with the speed of their own thoughts*, power to reveal themselves to men; and yet power to mingle and move among men unobserved and hidden."[71] (Italics added)

"Therefore," by these special powers and abilities, "great and marvelous works shall be wrought by them, before the great and coming day when all people must surely stand before the judgment-seat of Christ" (3 Ne. 28:31).

NOTE

1. Orson Pratt was ordained an apostle, under the hands of Oliver Cowdery, David Whitmer, and Martin Harris, on April 26, 1835, at age 23; excommunicated on August 20, 1842; rebaptized on January 20, 1843, and ordained to his former office in the Quorum of the Twelve Apostles. Brigham Young took him from his original position in the Quorum in 1875 and placed him in the order he would have been in when he was restored to fellowship had he come into the Quorum at that time. He died at Salt Lake City, Utah, on October 3, 1881, at age 70.

2. Brigham Young was ordained an apostle, under the hands of Oliver Cowdery, David Whitmer, and Martin Harris, on February 14, 1835, at age 33; sustained as President of the Quorum of the Twelve Apostles on April 14, 1840; sustained as the President of the Church on December 17, 1847, at age 46. He died at Salt Lake City, Utah, on August 19, 1877, at age 76.

3. Charles W. Penrose was ordained an apostle on July 7, 1904, by President Joseph F. Smith, at age 72; sustained as Second Counselor to President Smith on December 7, 1911, at age 79; sustained as Second Counselor to President Heber J. Grant on March 10, 1921. He died at Salt Lake City, Utah, on May 15, 1925, at age 93.

4. Anthony W. Ivins was ordained an apostle on October 6, 1907, by President Joseph F. Smith, at age 55; sustained as Second Counselor to President Heber J. Grant on March 10, 1921, at age 68; sustained as First Counselor to President Grant on May 28, 1925. He died at Salt Lake City, Utah on September 23, 1934, at age 82.

5. Melvin J. Ballard was ordained an apostle on January 7, 1919, by President Heber J. Grant, at age 45. He died at Salt Lake City, Utah on July 30, 1939, at age 66.

Chapter Eight

COMMENTS BY MEMBERS CONCERNING THE THREE NEPHITES

Many stories have been circulated among the Latter-day Saint people concerning appearances of The Three Nephites in modern times. Hundreds of these narratives are housed in folklore archives, located at various universities. When physically describing these special men, the stories vary greatly. Some people have described them as being old men, with white beards, gray beards, black beards, red beards, neat beards, and no beards at all. In addition, they are dressed in a variety of clothing. A few individuals have described them as being bent with age, while others describe them as standing as straight as an arrow. Most of the time, only one Nephite has performed a kind or wonderful deed. A few times, the three are together and have accomplished a great miracle.

Though these stories are highly interesting, it is very difficult, if not impossible, to verify the validity of each narrative. Therefore, only three stories told by early members of the Church will be presented in this chapter.

"ARMED FOR BATTLE"

This narrative is taken from Oliver B. Huntington's personal history. To refresh our memory, he is the same individual who wrote the names of the Three Nephites. His journal entry reads:

> *Friday, 13th Jan. 1881 . . . Brother James Bird was the person that Joseph Smith told of the 'three Nephites' at Far West.*
>
> *The matter relating to the Three Nephites was this: The morning that the Army of Governor Boggs exterminating order, attempted to come into Far West; Joseph the Prophet stood with the brethren behind the breast works so hastily thrown up in the night, and remarked as they were sweeping and swarming towards the beloved city; that if they came beyond a certain place, we would open fire upon them.*[72]

These statements, in part, are supported by what the Prophet wrote in the *Documentary History of the Church*:

> *On the 30th of October [1838] a large company of armed soldiers were seen approaching Far West . . . They had not yet got the governor's order of extermination, which I believe did not arrive till the next day.*
>
> Wednesday, October 31. – *The militia of Far West guarded the city the past night, and arranged a temporary fortification of wagons, timber, etc., on the south . . . The enemy was five to one against us.*[73]

With this information, we return to Brother Huntington's journal:

> The army came on, near the spot designated and on a sudden, they all turned and ran pel mell (sic) back to their camp, in great fright, declaring they saw too many thousands of soldiers to think of attacking the city.
>
> Joseph told Brother James Bird, 'that he saw between them and the mob one of the Three Nephites, with a drawn sword, before he made the remark about opening fire upon them, and when the mob had returned he saw the Three Nephites near the same place armed for battle.'
>
> The hosts that the 3 had with them, were undoubtedly exposed, by the power of God, to the view of the mob, being the hosts of soldiers they saw and fled from.[74]

Then, these comments are written in *A Comprehensive History of The Church*:

"There is some confusion as to the order of events for the next two or three days, owing to the annals on both sides being apparently defective by the omission or the confusion of some events that took place . . . on the evening of the 30th of October . . ."[75]

With this information, it is important to point out that some of the comments written by Brother Huntington are not supported by what Joseph Smith wrote in his history. Hence, the reader will have to determine whether or not the Prophet actually saw the Three Nephites, on the evening of October 30, 1838, "armed for battle."

THE MESSENGER GOING TO CUMORAH

This story was printed in the *Millennial Star*, an early publication of the Church. At that time, it was a common practice for the person who wrote the article to only write his or her initials. The following article was written and signed by E. S.:

While on their journey from Palmyra, Mr. [David] Whitmer relates a very interesting account of an aged appearing gentleman *on foot with a knapsack who came along-side of their wagon saying it is very warm, at the same time wiping his face. Mr. David asked him to take a ride. "Oh, no,' said he, 'I am only going over to Cumorah,' alluding to the hill Cumorah where the plates were shown to the prophet by the angel Moroni. Their mysterious visitor all of a sudden disappeared, and the country all around them was open. They very much marveled regarding the matter, insomuch as to ask Joseph [Smith], the prophet, to inquire of the Lord concerning their stranger. David said he looked around, for the prophet was riding behind sitting in the bed on some hay, and the prophet's face was nearly white and looked beautiful, his countenance fairly shone when he said that was* one of the Nephites *with the plates in the knapsack.*

After their arrival at Father Whitmers, David said that he had seen the same person, and subsequently his mother had the pleasure of seeing the distinguished Nephite, *who showed her the plates while turning over the golden leaves. On relating the circumstance she said that this was a portion of the plates fastened together, and these were those which were revealed, and not yet translated, but are to be after a time, and doubtless will reveal much useful knowledge when we are prepared to receive it. This is the only woman that I know of who was so favored as to behold those sacred writings, and I fully believe that this privilege was granted her as a special favor because of her kindness to the prophet of God, Joseph Smith.*[76]

Besides this story, there is a different version written in the *Doctrines And Covenants Commentary*. After the old man disappeared, it is written that David "Whitmer described his appearance and added, 'It was the messenger who had the plates [of the Book of Mormon], who had taken them from Joseph just prior to our starting for Harmony.'"[77]

This account gives the impression that the messenger was the Angel Moroni. In addition, there is no mention of David Whitmer's mother seeing the messenger or handling the golden plates. Therefore, from the article written in the *Millennial Star*, and the one published in the *Doctrine And Covenants Commentary*, the reader may surmise whether the messenger was the Angel Moroni or one of the Three Nephites. Likewise, it's the reader's opinion whether Mrs. Whitmer saw the messenger and handled the plates.

AN OLD MAN GAVE NEEDED MONEY

This missionary experience was printed in an early publication:

AUSTRALIA—1856 . . . we received a letter from Emue Plains, stating that the people would like to see and hear a 'Mormon' Elder. Emue Plains was a

distance of sixty miles from where we were, and
when we started, it had been raining about a week,
and a great portion of the country was flooded with
water. We had a large river to cross on the way, and
we were informed that the bridge had been carried
off and there was a ferry established across the river,
which charged five schillings each passenger. We did
not have any money with which to pay this charge,
and my companion was anxious to know what we
should do for money to pay the ferriage with. We
were then about three miles from the ferry, and were
passing through timber. I told him that we would go
into the woods and pray to God to open the heart of
some one to give it to us. We did so, and we had traveled but a short distance through a lane between two
fields, when we looked ahead of us a little way and we
saw an old man coming across the field. He came into
the road ahead of us, and as he came to meet us, he
had a smile on his countenance. He reached out his
hand to me, as if to shake hands, and left a crown, or
five shilling piece, in my hand and went to my
companion and did the same; but spoke not a word. I
cannot describe the feeling that we had when the man
took hold of our hands; we felt our hearts burn within
us, and it did not seem that we had power to ask him
his name or where he was from, as we usually did
when a person gave us any article of clothing or
money. He was about six feet high, well propor-
tioned, and wore a suit of light gray clothes and a
broad-brimmed hat, and his hair and beard were
about eighteen inches long and as white as snow. We
passed on and came to the ferry, and the money that
we had was just enough to pay our ferriage.[78]

Whether or not this "old man" was one of the Three Nephites, we are left to wonder. Once again, the reader may determine the validity of the narrative. No matter what we think about these three stories, it is important to realize that those early members seemed to truly believe what they wrote.

Chapter Nine

COMMENTS BY GENERAL AUTHORITIES CONCERNING THE THREE NEPHITES

"IN THEIR DREAMS"

In 1855, Elder Orson Pratt asked a congregation this searching question: "Do you suppose that these three Nephites have any knowledge of what is going on in this land?" Answering, he declared: "They know all about it; they are filled with the spirit of prophecy."[79]

Then, twenty years later, he revealed this information:

Forty-five years have passed away since God brought forth this sign, the Book of Mormon, *and sent missionaries to the nations . . . Now, after so long a period has elapsed since God brought forth this wonderful sign, he has begun to work among the remnants of the house of Israel, the American Indians, upon this [the American] continent, by his own power. What is it that has stirred them up to believe in this work? Has it been your exertion? Not altogether . . . Your hearts have been almost discouraged so far as your own labors were concerned. But how soon and how marvelously, when the time had come, has the Lord our God begun to operate upon them as nations and as tribes, bringing them in from hundreds of miles*

*distant to inquire after the Elders of this Church. What
for? What do they want with the Elders? They want to
be baptized. Who told them to come and be baptized?
They say that men came to them in their dreams, and
spoke to them in their own language, and told them
that away yonder was a people who had authority
from God to baptize them; but that they must repent of
their sins, cease their evil habits and lay aside the
traditions of their fathers, for they were false; that they
must cease to roam over the face of the land, robbing
and plundering . . .*

"*Who are these men who have been to the Indians
and told them to repent of their sins, and be baptized by
the 'Mormon?' They are men who obtained the promise
of the Lord, upwards of eighteen centuries ago, that
they should be instruments in his hands of bringing
about the redemption of their descendants.*[80]

Dreams and visions are closely related. As recorded in
the Book of Mormon, Lehi revealed this meaningful
doctrine: "Behold, I have dreamed a dream; or, in other
words, I have seen a vision" (1 Ne. 8: 2). From what Elder
Pratt said, those American Indians stated "that men came
to them in their dreams, and spoke to them in their own
language, and told them that away yonder was a people
who had authority from God to baptize them." Thus,
whether in dreams or visions or by personal appearances,
we find out that the Three Nephites have the ability to
"show themselves unto whatsoever man it seemeth them
good" (3 Ne. 28: 30).

"It Will Trouble You No More"

Among the many interesting incidents connected with our little home on the hillside," Elder Orson F. Whitney[81] says, *"there is one that should always be cherished by the members of my family. It will be better understood after reading what the Book of Mormon has to say upon the subject of the Three Nephites (3 Ne. 28: 4-30). My wife thus relates the incident:*

It happened many years ago. My husband was away, and the only members of the family in the house besides myself, were three of our little boys. It was early spring, and I was busy house-cleaning. Hearing the door-bell ring, I opened the door, and there stood an elderly man, with white hair and beard, clean, neatly dressed, straight as an arrow, and altogether respectable in appearance and respectful in manner. He carried a cane and held his hat in hand. He asked me if I could help him. I told him that I had no money, but if he needed food, I would gladly give him some. Said he: 'I would be very grateful.'

The unusual answer somewhat surprised me, but being much occupied, I paid slight attention. Showing him down into the dining room on the basement floor, I spread before him what food I had, and left him sitting at the table. The little boys were playing there at the time, and I told them to stay with the stranger and wait on him, while I returned to my work on the floor above.

After awhile I heard the patter of feet running up the stairs, and here came the boys, all breathless and excited, the oldest (Murray) exclaiming: 'Mama, I bet that was one of the Three Nephites!'

What makes you think so?' I inquired.

Here spoke up the second boy (Bert), who had had a toothache when the stranger arrived: 'I was holding my hand to my face, and he said,

'Son, what is troubling you?' 'My tooth aches,' I said. 'It will trouble you no more,' said he. And it stopped right then and hasn't ached since.'

The boys told me that the visitor, when departing by a back door, spoke these words: 'Peace be unto you and your house.' They likewise related how they rushed out after him, not seeing him pass the windows, and looked up and down the street and through the back yard, but could catch no glimpse of him . . . I have never been able to entirely banish the thought that possibly the boys were right.[82]

From this narrative, we may safely suppose that this elderly man was one of the Three Nephites who visited the Whitney home. By removing pain from a young boy suffering with a toothache, by simply saying, "It will trouble you no more," verifies the words written in the Book of Mormon: "Yea even among the Gentiles shall there be a great and marvelous work wrought by them, before that judgment day" (3 Ne. 28: 32).

ASKING FOR A VISIT FROM THE THREE NEPHITES

By assignment, Elder Heber J. Grant[83] traveled to Japan. The following missionaries accompanied him to that distant land—Louis B. Kelsch, Horace S. Ensign, and Alma O. Taylor. After they arrived and found suitable lodging, Elder Grant "felt the need to offer a special prayer, dedicating Japan for the preaching of the gospel. In this he was to follow a pattern that had been set long ago by his predecessors in the apostolic ministry.

"The day selected for the significant event was Sunday, September 1, 1901. The four missionaries found a secluded spot in the woods outside Yokohama and at about eleven o'clock they began their solemn meeting."[84]

We gather the following information from the journal of Elder Heber J. Grant:

> *After the prayer of dedication, we sang Sister Eliza R. Snow's inspired hymn 'O My Father Thou That Dwellest.' We first spoke and each expressed confidence and love for each other and the deepest gratitude for the privilege of being on this mission and more than once while the brethren were speaking, tears of gratitude filled my eyes for the rich outpouring of the good spirit which I felt in our midst. After singing Pres. Wilford Woodruff's favorite hymn 'God Moves In A Mysterious Way His Wonders to Perform,' Bro. Horace [S. Ensign] dismissed us. I have never in all my life enjoyed a little meeting more than I have the one we have had in the woods this day. I shall always remember the spot and it will be sacred in my memory to the day of my death. I never thought of such a thing as asking the Lord to allow the three Nephites to visit us, and aid in our work, but I hope and pray that we will live worthy of this part of my prayer being fulfilled. After our return from the woods, we had a little sacrament meeting and sang a number of sacrament hymns.*[85]

From Elder Grant, we discover that it is proper to ask

the Lord, based upon our worthiness, to allow the Three Nephites to aid us in our missionary work. Likewise, we can properly believe that they are willing to help us in this great cause. To support this belief, we read what Jesus said to those special men: ". . . and all this will I do because of the thing which ye have desired of me, for ye have desired that ye might bring the souls of men unto me, while the world shall stand" (3 Ne. 28: 9).

ARAB-ISRAELI CONFLICT

"Of interest is the following quotation from an article by Arthur U. Michelson," Elder LeGrand Richards[86] wrote, "which was published in 'The Jewish Hope,' Issue No. 9, Vol. 22, September, 1950.[87] The article suggests how the Lord may, even now, be fulfilling the prophecy of Zechariah, 'In that day shall the Lord defend the inhabitants of Jerusalem . . .':

> 'On my recent trip to Palestine I saw with my own eyes how God's prophecy is being fulfilled . . . It was marvelous what God did for the Jews, especially in Jerusalem, during the fighting with the Arabs . . . Everywhere I went I heard how God had intervened in their behalf . . .
>
> 'The Arabs, who had a great army in strong position, were determined to destroy the Jews, while the Jews were few in number, without any arms or ammunition. The two or three guns they possessed had to be rushed from one point to another, to give the Arabs the impression that they had many of them. The Jews had quite a few tin cans which they beat as they shot the

guns, giving the impression of many shots. But as the pressure was too great, they were unable to hold the lines any longer and finally decided to give up the city. At this critical moment God showed them that He was on their side, for He performed one of the greatest miracles that ever happened. The Arabs suddenly threw down their arms and surrendered. When their delegation appeared with the white flag, they asked, "Where are the three men that led you, and where are all the troops we saw?' The Jews told them that they did not know anything of the three men, for this group was their entire force. The Arabs said that they saw three persons with long beards and flowing white robes, who warned them not to fight any longer, otherwise they would all be killed. They became so frightened that they decided to give up. What an encouragement this was for the Jews, who realized that God was fighting for them.[88]

Then, Elder LeGrand Richards inserted these comments: "The Lord moves in a mysterious way His wonders to perform."[89] Two pages later, he wrote: "Therefore, 'the three persons with long beards and flowing white robes' could have been these three Nephite disciples (3 Ne. 28: 1-9; 27-31), for Jesus said: 'And behold they will be among the Gentiles, and the Gentiles shall know them not; they will also be among the Jews, and the Jews shall know them not.'"[90]

Besides this surrender, we learn of another. Elder Richards wrote:

We quote further from the article by Arthur U. Michelson: "God performed the same miracles on other fighting fronts, for He wanted to show the nations that he had turned to the Jews again, and like in the olden days, would help them to conquer the land. The Arabs were especially strong in the Negev District, not far from Beersheba, for they were backed by a large Egyptian army. The Jews were encircled by the Egyptians, and humanly speaking, had absolutely no chance to escape. One morning to the amazement of the Jews, the Arabs and the Egyptians suddenly gave up the fighting and surrendered. The Jews were at first very skeptical, because they couldn't believe that the Arabs and Egyptians would give up their strong position and surrender. But when they saw how the Arabs threw down their arms, they learned that God had intervened for them. When they asked the Arabs and Egyptians for the cause of their surrender, they told them that they saw an old man with a long beard who was dressed in a white robe, and who warned them not to fight any longer, otherwise they would all perish. This man was seen and heard by almost all the enemy troops. A great fear came over them and they decided to give up the fight. These and other stories I heard from various Jews who fought on the battle fronts . . .[91]

Again, Elder Richards added these comments:

"The man referred to 'with a long beard who was dressed in a white robe,' who warned the Arabs and Egyptians 'not to fight any longer, otherwise they would all be killed' could have been one of these Nephite disciples, or he could have been the Apostle John who was with the Savior in Jerusalem, for Jesus explained unto the three Nephite disciples that they desired of him the same thing 'which John, my beloved, who was with me in my ministry, before that I was lifted by the Jews, desired of me' (3 Nephi 28: 6)."[92]

"Fifty Years Before"

Some years ago, in 1959, with my wife, I came up from South and Central America to Mexico City and heard a testimony borne here. One of our elders told of meeting a woman seventy years of age in Tapachula in the state of Chiapas. When she was first visited by the elders, she almost immediately declared that she knew that what they taught was the truth. When she was asked how she knew, she declared that fifty years before, three elderly white-skinned men came into her hometown, and these three men preached the same doctrine that these elders were now preaching. These same men declared that in years to come other white-skinned missionaries would come and bring the true gospel of Jesus Christ and they should accept it.[93]

I had previously listened to missionaries in Mexico, who reported that they had likewise found people in their land who said the same thing.[94]

These remarks by President Harold B. Lee confirm the words written by Mormon: "And it shall come to pass, when the Lord seeth fit in his wisdom that they shall minister unto all the scattered tribes of Israel, and unto all nations, kindreds, tongues and people, and shall bring out of them unto Jesus many souls, that their desire may be fulfilled, and also because of the convincing power of God which is in them" (3 Ne. 28: 29).

Because they are the Lord's chosen servants, these four comments demonstrate that the Three Nephites are truly aiding the work of the Lord upon this earth. In addition, they support the words written by Mormon: "Therefore, more blessed are ye, for ye shall never taste of death; but ye shall live to behold all the doings of the Father unto the children of men, even until all things shall be fulfilled according to the will of the Father, when I shall come in my glory with the powers of heaven" (3 Ne. 28: 7).

NOTES

1. Orson F. Whitney was ordained an apostle on April 9, 1906, by President Joseph F. Smith, at age 50; he died May 16, 1931, at Salt Lake City, Utah, at age 75.

2. Heber J. Grant was ordained an apostle on October 16, 1882, by George Q. Cannon, at age 25; he became the President of the Quorum of the Twelve Apostles on November 23, 1916; ordained and set apart as the President of the Church, November 23, 1918, at age 62; he died May 14, 1945, at Salt Lake City, Utah, at age 88.

3. LeGrand Richards was sustained as the Presiding Bishop of the Church on April 6, 1938, at age 52; ordained an apostle, April 10, 1952, by President David O. McKay, at age 66; he died January 11, 1983, at Salt Lake City, Utah, at age 96.

4. "The story was first published in September 1950 by Arthur U. Michelson in a Los Angeles newspaper called *The Jewish Hope* and was picked up and passed into Mormon tradition by Joseph Fielding Smith in *The Signs of the Times: A Series of Discussions* (Salt Lake City: Deseret News Press, 1952), pp. 227-33, and by LeGrand Richards in *Israel! Do You Know* (Salt Lake City: Deseret Book Company, 1954), pp. 229-33, and in "The Word of Our God Will Stand," *Improvement Era* 57 (June 1954): 404-6. For a possible source of this story, see Dov Joseph, *The Faithful City: Siege of Jerusalem*, 1948 (New York: Simon and Schuster, 1960), p. 73." These comments were written in Dialogue—A Journal Of Mormon Thought, Vol. 21, No. 3, Autumn 1988, from an article by William A. Wilson, *Freeways, Parking Lots, and Ice Cream Stands: The Three Nephites in Contemporary Society.*

5. Harold B. Lee was ordained an apostle on April 10, 1941, by President Heber J. Grant, at age 42; sustained as the President of the Quorum of the Twelve Apostles, January 23, 1970; sustained as First Counselor to President Joseph Fielding Smith, January 23, 1970; ordained and set apart as the President of the Church, July 7, 1972, at age 73; he died on December 26, 1973, at Salt Lake City, Utah, at age 74.

Chapter Ten

CITY OF ENOCH
(Moses 7)

From the writings of Moses, we find out that Enoch and the inhabitants of the holy city he built were the first people to be translated. We further learn that Enoch was a spiritual giant. His faith was so great that when he spoke the word of the Lord, the "earth trembled, and the mountains fled," and the "rivers of water were turned out of their course," and "all nations feared greatly, so powerful was the word of Enoch, and so great was the power of the language which God had given him" (7: 13).

So righteous were the citizens who associated with Enoch, that the "Lord came and dwelt with his people, and they dwelt in righteousness" (7: 16). The record further states: "And the Lord called his people Zion, because they were of one heart and one mind, and dwelt in righteousness; and there was no poor among them" (7: 18).

As to the ministry of this great seer, we read: "And Enoch continued his preaching in righteousness unto the people of God. And it came to pass in his days, that he built a city that was called the City of Holiness, even Zion" (7: 19). Later in the scriptural account, we read these meaningful words: "And all the days of Zion, in the days of Enoch, were three hundred and sixty-five years.

"And Enoch and all his people walked with God, and

he dwelt in the midst of Zion; and it came to pass that Zion was not, for God received it up into his own bosom; and from thence went forth the saying, Zion is Fled" (7: 68-69).

Why were the inhabitants of the City of Enoch translated and taken from this earth? All of them were too righteous, too holy to remain upon this carnal and wicked world.

> *After those in the City of Holiness were translated and taken up into heaven without tasting death, so that Zion as a people and a congregation had fled from the battle-scarred surface of the earth, the Lord sought others among men who would serve him. From the days of Enoch to the flood, new converts and true believers, except those needed to carry out the Lord's purposes among mortals, were translated, "and the Holy Ghost fell on many, and they were caught up by the powers of heaven into Zion." (Moses 7: 27). "And men having this faith—the faith of Enoch and his people—"coming up unto this order of God—the holy order of priesthood which we call the Melchizedek Priesthood—"were translated and taken up into heaven" (JST, Gen. 14: 32).*
>
> —Elder Bruce R. McConkie[95]

Elder McConkie then explains that after the flood, "except in a few special cases—those of Moses, Elijah, Alma the son of Alma, John the Beloved, and the Three Nephites are the only ones of which we know—each involving a special purpose, the Lord ceased translating faithful people. Rather, they were permitted to die and go into the spirit world, there to perform the ever-increasing work needed in that sphere."[96]

Turning our attention to Enoch and the citizens of his holy city, President Brigham Young declared: "Enoch was the only man that could build a city to God; and as soon as he had it completed, *he and his city, with its walls, houses, land, rivers, and everything pertaining to it, were taken away.*"[97] (Italics added)

In harmony with this statement, President Heber C. Kimball, First Counselor to President Brigham Young, said: "Because there was such a oneness among the people of Enoch, and they could not continue to be one, and live with the people in the same world, *God took them and their city with a part of this earth to himself, and they sailed away like one ship at sea separating from another.*"[98] (Italics added)

A year later, President Kimball stated: ". . . if we will take a course as a people to listen to counsel, and do as we are told, and all the nations of the earth were to come upon us, and there was no other way for our deliverance, God would break this portion of the earth off, and take us away as he did Enoch. He took Enoch away on a portion of the earth, and cannot he break another portion off and take us away? He took them away because they were determined to serve the Lord, and he would do the same for us."[99]

LOCATION OF THE CITY OF ENOCH

To find where the City of Enoch was located, we read these informative words, as recorded by Elder Wilford Woodruff: "President [Brigham] Young said 'Joseph the Prophet told me . . . *that when the City of Enoch fled and was translated it was where the gulf of Mexico now is.* It left that gulf a body of water.'"[100] (Italics added)

In addition to Elder Woodruff's journal entry, we read what President George Q. Cannon,[101] First Counselor to President John Taylor, wrote in *The Juvenile Instructor*: "The Prophet Brigham Young is authority for the belief that the city which Enoch built and the earth upon which it stood *formerly occupied that portion which is now called the Gulf of Mexico.* This is the general view taken by the leading Elders of the Church . . . ."[102] (Italics added)

In a published book, Leon M. Strong says: "Orson F. Whitney told the writer in 1933 that his mother told him that the City of Enoch was once where the Gulf of Mexico now is. Elder Whitney said his mother got this from the Prophet Joseph and that he (Elder Whitney) had mentioned it in a sermon he preached in Salt Lake City while bishop of a ward there. He said he had also preached the same thought after becoming a member of the Quorum of the Twelve."[103]

As to where this translated city was taken, Elder Orson Pratt penned this view: "However far the Zion of Enoch may be from the earth's appointed orbit, it is certain, according to the promise of God, that it will return again to the earth at the second coming of Christ. We can hardly believe that this city was taken away beyond the limits of the Solar system; for if it had been carried with a velocity of one mile per minute, it would have required upwards of five thousand years to have gone as far as the planet Neptune: and with that velocity it would have required over ten thousand years to go there and return. *As an immortal body has the power of rendering itself invisible, it is reasonable to infer that a city wrought upon by the power of God, and changed in its nature, could be rendered invisible, and still be within our immediate vicinity.*"[104] (Italics added)

Concerning the inhabitants of this holy city, Elder Harold B. Lee expressed these thought-provoking comments: "I walked over to the Church Office Building with President Joseph Fielding Smith and he said, 'I believe there has never been a moment of time since the creation but what there has been someone holding the priesthood on the earth to hold Satan in check.' And then I thought of Enoch's city with perhaps thousands who were taken into heaven and were translated. They must have been translated for a purpose *and may have sojourned with those living on the earth ever since that time.*"[105] (Italics added)

From what has been spoken by early Church leaders, we know that Enoch's city, with its walls, houses, land, rivers, and everything pertaining to it, was taken away from the earth. Whether it is near or far from this world, we are not informed. From what has been revealed, we know that translated beings can show themselves to whomever they desire. Because Enoch's city was physically taken from this earth, it appears more likely that those holy inhabitants may have visited—instead of sojourned—with those living on the earth ever since the time of their translation.

NOTE

1. George Q. Cannon was ordained an apostle on August 26, 1860,

by President Brigham Young, at age 33; he was sustained as a counselor to President Young, April 8, 1873, at age 46; he was sustained as assistant counselor to President Young on May 9, 1874; he was released at the death of President Young on August 28, 1877; sustained as First Counselor to President John Taylor on October 10, 1880; released at the death of President Taylor on July 25, 1887; he was sustained as First Counselor to President Wilford Woodruff on April 7, 1889; he was sustained as First Counselor to President Lorenzo Snow on September 13, 1898; he died on April 12, 1901, at Monterey, California, at age 74.

Chapter Eleven

MELCHIZEDEK AND HIS CITY OF PEACE
(JST Genesis 14; D&C 107: Alma 13)

In spiritual stature, Melchizedek was like unto Enoch. As the Joseph Smith Translation of Genesis says: "Now Melchizedek was a man of faith, who wrought righteousness; and when a child he feared God, and stopped the mouths of lions, and quenched the violence of fire. And thus, having been approved of God, he was ordained an high priest after the order of the covenant which God made with Enoch, it being after the order of the Son of God; which order came, not by man, nor the will of man; neither by father nor mother; neither by beginning of days nor end of years; but of God; and it was delivered unto men by the calling of his own voice, according to his own will, unto as many as believed on his name" (JST, Gen. 14: 26-29).

Concerning this order of the Son of God, we discover that Melchizedek was ordained a high priest by the order of the priesthood. Thus, this great man did not ordain himself to be a high priest; another priesthood holder performed this ordination.

As it pertains to Melchizedek, the Prophet Joseph Smith revealed this doctrine:

There are, in the church, two priesthoods, namely,

the Melchizedek and Aaronic, including the Levitical Priesthood. Why the first is called the Melchizedek Priesthood is because Melchizedek was such a great high priest. Before his day it was called the Holy Priesthood, after the Order of the Son of God. But out of respect or reverence to the name of the Supreme Being, to avoid the too frequent repetition of his name, they, the church, in ancient days, called that priesthood after Melchizedek, or the Melchizedek Priesthood. All other authorities or offices in the church are appendages to this priesthood (D&C 107: 1-5).

In the *Book of Mormon*, Alma tells us that "Melchizedek was a king over the land of Salem; and his people had waxed strong in iniquity and abomination; yea, they had all gone astray; they were full of all manner of wickedness; But Melchizedek having exercised mighty faith, and received the office of the high priesthood according to the holy order of God, did preach repentance unto his people. And behold, they did repent; and Melchizedek did establish peace in the land in his days; therefore he was called the prince of peace, for he was the king of Salem; and he did reign under his father" (Alma 13: 17-18).

Then, from Elder McConkie we gather this information: "Anciently Jerusalem was appointed by the Lord to be the *City of Peace*. The name itself apparently derives from the Hebrew *shalom* (*shalem*) meaning *peace*. Melchizedek was king of Salem, and like Enoch, whose converts worshipped the Lord in the *City of Holiness*, so the converts of Melchizedek worshipped in the *City of Peace* where Melchizedek reigned as the Prince of Peace (JST, Gen. 14: 33)."[106]

With this knowledge, we repeat what Elder McConkie wrote in the previous chapter concerning the City of Enoch:

> *After those in the City of Holiness were translated and taken up into heaven without tasting death, so that Zion as a people and a congregation had fled from the battle-scarred surface of the earth, the Lord sought others among men who would serve him. From the days of Enoch to the flood, new converts and true believers, except those needed to carry out the Lord's purposes among mortals, were translated, "and the Holy Ghost fell on many, and they were caught up by the powers of heaven into Zion" (Moses 7: 27). "And men having this faith"—the faith of Enoch and his people—"coming up unto this order of God"—the holy order of priesthood which we call the Melchizedek Priesthood—'were translated and taken up into heaven' (JST, Gen. 14: 32).*[107]

Then, from the Joseph Smith Translation of Genesis, we find out what happened to Melchizedek and his faithful converts: "And now, Melchizedek was a priest of this order; therefore he obtained peace in Salem, and was called the Prince of Peace. *And his people wrought righteousness, and obtained heaven, and sought for the city of Enoch which God had before taken*, separating it from the earth, having reserved it unto the latter days, or the end of the world; And hath said, and sworn with an oath, that the heavens and the earth should come together; and the sons of God should be tried so as by fire" (13: 33-35). (Italics added)

"But thereafter," Elder McConkie says, "except in a few isolated instances—those of Moses, Elijah, Alma the son of Alma, John the Beloved, and the Three Nephites are the only ones of which we know—except in these cases, each involving a special purpose, the Lord ceased translating faithful people."[108]

From these expressions, we may safely believe that Melchizedek and those righteous people who lived in the City of Peace were translated. However, we are not informed as to whether any land or houses were translated with them.

Chapter Twelve

MOSES AND ELIJAH
(Deut. 34; 2 Kings 2; Alma 45; D&C 110)

Both Moses and Elijah were mighty prophets of God. The miracles attending their respective ministries have rarely been duplicated. As translated beings, they appeared on the Mount of Transfiguration and, with our Lord, they restored keys upon Peter, James, and John.[109] Then, as resurrected beings, they appeared to the Prophet Joseph Smith and Oliver Cowdery in the Kirtland Temple and committed unto them keys.

Concerning the death of Moses, as recorded in the Old Testament, Brother Charles W. Penrose said:

> "So Moses the servant of the Lord died there in the land of Moab, according to the word of the Lord. And he buried him in a valley in the land of Moab, over against Bethpeor: but no man knoweth of his sepulcher unto this day" (Deut. 34: 5-6).
>
> Do you think God revealed that? I am satisfied He did not. The person who revised these books added that by way of explanation. How do they know he died, or how do they know the Lord buried him? They simply learned that Moses went out of the midst of the people; they did not know what became of him; so they supposed he died and that the Lord buried him, because nobody else had done so. "No man knoweth his

sepulcher unto this day." No wonder; because he did not have any sepulcher. According to what we have learned [as Latter-day Saints], he was treated the same as Elijah was; not taken up in a chariot of fire perhaps, but translated, quickened by the power of God, that he might remain as a witness of the Lord unto the last day. He appeared with Elijah to Jesus in the Mount of Transfiguration. It is appointed unto all men once to die; but some men have been translated, as it was in the days of Enoch, and they will like others pass through the great change.[110]

In harmony with these comments, President Brigham Young stated: "It may be said that Enoch and his holy city went to heaven, that Elijah was caught up, *and that it is generally believed* [by the Latter-day Saint people] *that Moses did not die*; still that sentence [of death] that is passed upon all mankind will come upon them at some time or other. They must meet this change, to be prepared to enter into the celestial kingdom of our Father and God."[111] (Italics added)

Regarding President Young's comment "that Elijah was caught up," we read that Elijah called Elisha to follow him, and as they "talked, that, behold, there appeared a chariot of fire, and horses of fire . . . and Elijah went up by a whirlwind into heaven. And Elisha saw it . . ." (2 Kings 2: 11-12).

"Now, there was a *reason* for the translation of Elijah." Elder Joseph Fielding Smith says, "*Men are not preserved in that manner unless there is a reason for it.* Moses was likewise taken up, though the scriptures say that the Lord buried him upon the mountain. Of course, the writer of that wrote according to his understanding; but *Moses, like Elijah, was taken up without tasting death, because he had a mission to perform . . .*"[112] (Italics added)

As to why they appeared on the Mount of Transfiguration as translated beings, Elder Smith provided this explanation:

> . . . *Elijah and Moses were preserved from death: because they had a mission to perform, and it had to be performed before the crucifixion of the Son of God, and it could not be done in the spirit. They had to have tangible bodies. Christ is the first fruits of the resurrection; therefore if any former prophets had a work to perform preparatory to the mission of the Son of God, or to the dispensation of the meridian of times, it was essential that they be preserved to fulfill that mission in the flesh. For that reason Moses disappeared from among the people and was taken up into the mountain, and the people thought he was buried by the Lord. The Lord preserved him, so that he could come at the proper time and restore his keys, on the heads of Peter, James, and John, who stood at the head of the dispensation of the meridian of time. He reserved Elijah from death that he might also come and bestow his keys upon the heads of Peter, James, and John and prepare them for their ministry.*
>
> *But, one says, the Lord could have waited until after his resurrection, and then they could have done it. It is quite evident, due to the fact that it did so occur, that it had to be done before; and there was a reason. There may have been other reasons, but that is one reason why Moses and Elijah did not suffer death in the flesh, like other men do.*[113]

As to what happened to Elijah and Moses, following the death of our Lord, we again turn to Elder Smith for understanding: "After the resurrection of Christ, of course, they passed through death and the resurrection, and then as *resurrected beings* came to fulfill a mission of like import in the dispensation of the fulness of time (D&C 110: 11-16; 133: 54-55)."[114]

Therefore, Moses and Elijah were first translated because they had an important mission to perform upon the Mount of Transfiguration with tangible bodies. Secondly, they passed through death and the resurrection, and each appeared to the Prophet Joseph Smith and Oliver Cowdery, on April 3, 1836, in the Kirtland Temple and restored important keys.

Chapter Thirteen

JOHN THE BELOVED
(John 21: 18-25)

Briefly repeating what has been previously written in Chapter Five of this work, we find out that as our Lord and the senior apostle walked together, Peter, "turning about," saw John—curious as to what would happen to his close colleague and friend—and asked: "Lord, and what shall this man do?"

Jesus answered, "If I will that he tarry till I come, what is that to thee?" He further told Peter: "Follow thou me." The beloved apostle also wrote: "Then went this saying abroad among the brethren, that [John] should not die."

John's own account of his translation was revealed to the Prophet Joseph Smith. As it pertains to our Savior's words to the senior apostle, we read: "And for this cause the Lord said unto Peter: If I will that he tarry till I come, what is that to thee? For he desired of me that he might bring souls unto me, but thou desiredst that thou mightest speedily come unto me in my kingdom. I say unto thee, Peter, this was a good desire; but my beloved has desired that he might do more, or a greater work yet among men than what he has before done." Then, regarding the three, presiding apostles, the Lord further stated: "Yea, he [John] has undertaken a greater work; therefore I will make him as flaming fire and a ministering angel; he shall minister for those who shall be heirs of salvation who dwell on the earth. And I will make thee [Peter] to minister for him [John] and for [his] brother James; and unto you three I will give this power and the keys of this ministry until I come. Verily I say unto you [Peter], ye shall both [Peter and John] have according to your desires, for ye both joy in that which ye have desired." (D&C 7: 4-8)[115]

"That John still lives in the embodied state," says Elder Talmage, "and shall remain in the flesh until the Lord's yet future advent, is attested by later revelation. In company with his martyred and resurrected companions, Peter and James, and the 'disciple whom Jesus loved' has officiated in the restoration of the Holy Apostleship in this the dispensation of the fulness of times."[116]

In support of Elder Talmage's statement, Elder Wilford Woodruff stated, "The first quorum of Apostles were all put to death, *except John, and we are informed that he still remains on the earth*, though his body had doubtless undergone some change."[117] (Italics added)

As to John's continual ministry in this dispensation, we quote again from Oliver B. Huntington's personal history. To refresh our memory, he is the same individual who wrote the names of the Three Nephites. His journal entry reads:

> *Friday, 13th JAN. 1881 . . . While 'the camp of Zion' was on the way to Missouri in 1834, Joseph was some ways ahead of the company one day, when there was seen talking with him by the roadside a man, a stranger. When the company came up there was no person with him. When at camp that night, Heber [C. Kimball] asked the Prophet who that man was; Joseph*

replied it was the beloved Disciple, John, who was then on his way to the ten tribes in the North.

I have heard Joseph say that "John was among the ten tribes beyond the north pole."[118]

In his history dated Tuesday, May 27, 1834, Joseph Smith wrote that while their enemies were constantly threatening acts of violence, the members of the camp did not fear, neither did they hesitate to continue their journey, "for God was with us, and His angels went before us."[119] Though the Prophet does not state that he saw the beloved disciple, he does say: "We know that angels were our companions, for we saw them."[120]

From the scriptures, and the writings of General Authorities, we are informed that the Apostle John is sometimes designated as the beloved disciple. Also, he is designated as the Revelator.

At the fourth General Conference of the Church, held in Kirtland, Ohio, in June of 1831, "The Spirit of the Lord fell upon Joseph in an unusual manner, and he prophesied that *John the Revelator* was then *among the Ten Tribes of Israel . . .*"[121] (Italics added)

Therefore, three years prior to the march of Zion's camp, the Prophet stated that John was among the Ten Tribes of Israel. Thus, we are left to wonder if Brother's Huntington's journal entry is correct. If it is correct, perhaps John was making another visit to the Ten Tribes?

Besides visiting the Ten Tribes, we may be assured that John the Revelator—like the Three Nephites—ministers "unto all the scattered tribes of Israel, and unto all nations, kindreds, tongues and people," and continues to "bring out of them unto Jesus many souls" (3 Ne. 28: 29). To support this belief, we repeat what our Lord told Peter in the Old World, "If I will that he [John] tarry till I come, what is that to thee? *For he desired of me that he might bring souls unto me . . .*" Further, ". . . *my beloved has desired that he might do more, or a greater work yet among men than what he has before done . . .* therefore I will make him as flaming fire and a ministering angel; he shall minister for those who shall be heirs of salvation *who dwell on the earth*" (D&C 7: 4-6). (Italics added)

Chapter Fourteen

ALMA THE YOUNGER
(Mosiah 27-29)

Unlike Enoch, Melchizedek, Moses, and Elijah, we find out that Alma, who was the son of Alma, was at first "numbered among the unbelievers." Though his father was the high priest over the Church, Alma—who is commonly referred to as *Alma the younger*—became a "very wicked and idolatrous man." Briefly describing what transpired in his early life, we turn to Dr. Sidney B. Sperry for information:

> *Among the unbelievers in the land of Zarahemla was the wicked and idolatrous Alma, one of the sons of the elder Alma. He seemed to have been a suave and eloquent young man, who became a great hindrance to the Church by speaking flattery to the people and stirring up dissension. In this he was aided and abetted by the four sons of Mosiah: Ammon, Aaron, Omner and Himni. This quintet [this group of five] went secretly about the land seeking to destroy the Church and lead the Lord's people astray.*
> *On one occasion, as they were going about doing the devil's work, an angel of God appeared to them and spoke with a voice of thunder, which caused the earth to shake. He addressed his words to Alma, who seems to have been the ringleader of the group, and reproved*

*him by asking why he persecuted the Church of God.
The divine messenger announced that he had come in
response to the prayers of the Lord's people and to the
prayers of the elder Alma, his father. He reminded
Alma of the great things that the Lord had done for his
fathers and directed him to go his way and seek no
more to destroy the Church. Having given his message,
the angel departed.*[122]

After Alma's miraculous conversion, he bore a strong
testimony of the divinity of the Savior, and "began from
this time forward to teach the people, and those who were
with Alma at the time the angel appeared unto them, traveling round about through all the land, publishing to all
the people the things which they had heard and seen, and
preaching the word of God in much tribulation . . ." (27:
32).

As time went on, king Mosiah "took the plates of brass,
and all the things which he had kept, and conferred them
upon Alma, who was the son of Alma . . . and commanded
him that he should keep and preserve them, and also keep
a record of the people, handing them down from one
generation to another . . ." (28: 20).

"And it came to pass that Alma was appointed to be the
first chief judge, he being also the high priest, his father
having conferred the office upon him, and having given
him the charge concerning all the affairs of the church"
(29: 42).

After being chief judge for eight years, Alma delivered
the judgeship to Nephihah and devoted his time to the
work of the ministry (Alma 1-4).

Alma counseled each of his sons, Helaman, Shiblon,
and Corianton, to be valiant in their testimonies (Alma 36-
42). Helaman was entrusted with the records and sacred

relics (Alma 37: 1-5). After blessing his sons, Alma "blessed the church, yea, all those who should stand fast in the faith from that time henceforth" (Alma 45: 17).

THE TRANSLATION OF ALMA
(Alma 45)

"And when Alma had done this he departed out of the land of Zarahemla, as if to go into the land of Melek. *And it came to pass that he was never heard of more; as to his death or burial we know not of*" (45: 18). (Italics added)

Then, the great historian, Mormon, added this significant comment:

"Behold, this we know, that he was a righteous man; *and the saying went abroad in the church that he was taken up by the Spirit, or buried by the hand of the Lord, even as Moses. But behold, the scriptures saith the Lord took Moses unto himself; and we suppose that he has also received Alma in the spirit, unto himself*; therefore, for this cause we know nothing concerning his death and burial" (45: 19). (Italics added)

After quoting this scripture, Elder Joseph Fielding Smith penned these words: "It is a very reasonable thought to believe that both Moses and *Alma*, like Elijah and John [the Revelator], *were translated* to accomplish some work which the Lord had in store for them at some future day."[123] (Italics added)

In declarative words, Elder Bruce R. McConkie says, "Moses, Elijah, and *Alma the younger, were translated*."[124] (Italics added)

As to the mission he accomplished there has been unsupported speculation, by a few members of the

Church, that Alma was one of the wise men who visited the baby Jesus in the Old World. The only information we have is that this righteous man was translated to accomplish the work of the Lord.

Chapter Fifteen

NEPHI
(The Book of Helaman)

A great Nephite missionary was Nephi, who is designated as the second Nephi, who was the son of the third Helaman.[125] After the death of his father, Nephi became the chief judge. "And it came to pass that he did fill the judgment-seat with justice and equity; yea, he did keep the commandments of God, and did walk in the ways of his father" (3: 37).

After serving for several years in this position, "Nephi delivered up the judgment-seat to a man whose name was Cezoram" (5: 1). Nephi "yielded up the judgement-seat, and took it upon him to preach the word of God all the remainder of his days, and his brother Lehi also, all the remainder of his days" (5: 4). So successful were they in their missionary service that eight thousand Lamanites were converted (5: 18-19). While in the land of Nephi, these brothers were cast into prison. Great spiritual manifestations occurred and they were released from bondage. Because of these manifestations, and the testimony of about three hundred souls who witnessed these great happenings, the majority of Lamanites were converted (5: 49-52).

Later in his ministry, Nephi was greatly discouraged "because of the wickedness of the people of the Nephites, their secret works of darkness, and their murderings, and their plunderings, and all manner of iniquities—and it came to pass as he was thus pondering in his heart, behold, a voice came unto him saying:

"Blessed art thou, Nephi, for those things which thou has done . . . behold, I will bless thee forever; and I will make thee mighty in word and in deed, in faith and in works; yea, even that all things shall be done unto thee according to thy word, for thou shalt not ask that which is contrary to my will."

This voice further declared, "Behold, thou art Nephi, and I am God. Bold, I declare it unto thee in the presence of mine angels, that ye shall have power over this people, and shall smite the earth with famine, and with pestilence, and destruction, according to the wickedness of this people.

"Behold, I give unto you power, that whatsoever ye shall seal on earth shall be sealed in heaven . . ." (10: 3-7).

The Lord then commanded Nephi to go forth again and tell the people to repent or they would be smitten unto destruction. Without going home, this great prophet immediately did as the Lord instructed.

"But behold, the power of God was with him, and they could not take him to cast him into prison, for he was taken by the Spirit and conveyed away out of the midst of them . . . thus he did go forth in the Spirit, from multitude to multitude, declaring the word of God, even until he had declared it unto them all, or sent it forth among all the people" (10: 16-17).

It has been falsely written that Nephi the son of Helaman was "apparently" a translated being at this time in order to be taken by the Spirit from multitude to multitude. To help clarify, Elder McConkie has written that at different times, Ezekiel, Nephi the son of Lehi, Mary the mother of Jesus, Nephi the son of Helaman, and Philip were 'transported bodily' from one place to another by the Spirit."[126] And, the Joseph Smith Translation of Luke 4: 9 states that "the Spirit (not the devil) brought (Jesus) to Jerusalem, and set him on a pinnacle of the temple." From these illustrations, it is obvious that an individual can be bodily transported by the spirit and NOT be a translated being.

Continuing with the record, we read that wars and contentions developed in the land. The Gadianton robbers caused so much destruction and wickedness, that Nephi decided to use the powers he was promised. He prayed to the Lord and asked him not destroy the people by the sword, but cause a famine to turn them to repentance (11: 1-4).

A great famine came, and for over two years the land became so dry that it did not produce grain, and thousands of people perished. When the people saw that they were about to perish by famine, they began to remember God, and the words spoken by Nephi. They pleaded with their chief judges and their leaders that they would speak unto Nephi and tell him that they knew he was a man of God, and to ask the Lord to turn away the famine. The judges did as requested. When Nephi saw that the people had repented, he prayed unto the Lord and asked him to turn away his anger and see if the people would serve him. This prayer was effective, and once more rain fell and the earth brought forth its fruits and grains. The people esteemed Nephi as a great prophet, and as a man of God. Peace prevailed in the land and most of the people, both Nephites and Lamanites, did belong to the church (11: 1-21).

DISAPPEARANCE OF NEPHI
(3 Nephi 1)

We now advance to the time when the ninety-first year of the reign of judges had passed away, and it was six hundred years from the time that Lehi had left Jerusalem. Nephi entrusted to his eldest son, Nephi (who later became the head of the Nephite Twelve Apostles), the plates of brass, and all the sacred records, together with all those sacred relics that had been brought out of Jerusalem.

"Then he departed out of the land, *and whither he went, no man knoweth . . .*" (1: 1-3). (Italics added)

"This strange disappearance," Dr. Sperry says, "of such a great spiritual character merits more than passing notice. Little attention might be paid to the incident were it not for the fact that the younger Alma disappeared under somewhat similar circumstances after delivering up the records to his son Helaman (Alma 37: 1-5; 45: 17-19). What happened to Nephi? Was he slain under mysterious circumstances and his body never recovered, *or was he translated?* We are not specifically told, but one gets the distinct impression that some great spiritual incident lies behind the disappearance of Nephi."[127] (Italics added)

Though it has not be officially stated by the leaders of the Church, several members of the Church believe that

Nephi was translated, as was Alma the younger. Again, there has been unsupported speculation, by some members of the Church, that Nephi—like Alma the younger—was one of the wise men that visited the baby Jesus in the Old World. The only information we have is that this righteous man "departed out of the land, and whither he went, no man knoweth."

NOTE

1. In the heading of Chapter 2 of the Book of Helaman, it states that "Helaman the second becomes chief judge." This is verified by what is written in verse two. However, to distinguish those individuals named Helaman, the Index of the *Book of Mormon* designates him as the third Helaman. The author has used the numbering system as designated in the Index.

Chapter Sixteen

ETHER
(Book of Ether)

Relying upon Dr. Sperry for knowledge, we gather this information: "The Book of Ether may be analyzed under three major headings as follows:

"I. Early history of the Jaredite people before coming to this (the American) continent (Chs. 1-4) . . .

"II. Moroni writes to future translator of his writings (Ch. 5) . . .

"III. History of Jaredite people from the time they set sail for the promised land until their final destruction as a nation. With commentaries and admonitions by Moroni (Chs. 6-15)."[128]

In this record, we find out that *"Ether was a prophet of the Lord*; wherefore Ether came forth in the days of [king] Coriantumr, and began to prophecy unto the people, for he could not be restrained because of the Spirit of the Lord which was in him. For he did cry from the morning, even until the going down of the sun, exhorting the people to believe in God unto repentance lest they should be destroyed . . . And it came to pass that Ether did prophesy great and marvelous things unto the people, which they did not believe, because they saw them not" (12: 1-5). (Italics added)

Speaking of faith, Moroni wrote the following

commentary: "And it was by faith that the three [Nephite] disciples obtained a promise that they should not taste of death; and they obtained not the promise until after their faith" (12: 17).

Continuing, he spoke of others who were blessed because of their great faith: "And there were many whose faith was so exceedingly strong, even before Christ came, who could not be kept from within the veil, but truly saw with their eyes the things which they had beheld with an eye of faith, and they were glad" (12: 19).

One of those spiritually attuned individuals was the brother of Jared. This righteous man saw the finger of the Lord as he touched sixteen stones. So great was the brother of Jared's faith that the pre-mortal Christ showed himself unto him and told him that he was redeemed from the fall [of Adam and Eve]; therefore, he was brought back into the Lord's presence (Ch. 3).

Turning our attention to what transpired in Ether's ministry, we find out that "in the second year the word of the Lord came to Ether, that he should go and prophesy unto Coriantumr that, if he would repent, and all his household, the Lord would give unto him his kingdom and spare the people—Otherwise they should be destroyed, and all his household save it were himself" (13: 20-21).

The record informs us that "Coriantumr repented not, neither his household, neither the people; and the wars ceased not; and they sought to kill Ether, but he fled from before them and hid again in the cavity of the rock" (13: 22).

"And it came to pass that the people began to flock together in armies, throughout all the face of the land. And they were divided; and a part of them fled to the army of Shiz, and a part of them fled to the army of Coriantumr.

And so great and lasting had been the war, and so long had been the scene of bloodshed and carnage, that the whole face of the land was covered with the bodies of the dead" (14: 19-21).

So destructive was this war, Coriantumr wrote an epistle to Shiz asking him to take the kingdom and spare the people, but no agreement was made. After millions of people had been slain, only Shiz and Coriantumr survived the battle. After resting for a little, the king cut off the head of his vindictive enemy, who had fainted from the loss of blood. As Ether had prophesied, Coriantumr was the only survivor—excepting Ether—of that great Jaredite nation (15: 2, 15-32).

"When the struggle was over," Dr. Sperry says, "the Lord told Ether to go forth. He did so and found that the Lord's words had been completely fulfilled. After finishing his record, he hid the plates where the people of Limhi found them (Mosiah 8: 7-9). For some reason or other Moroni felt inspired to record the very last words which were written by Ether. Here they are:

> . . . *Whether the Lord will that I be translated, or that I suffer the will of the Lord in the flesh, it mattereth not, if it so be that I am saved in the kingdom of God. Amen (15: 34).* (Italics added)

"Why did Moroni quote the last words of Ether? Is it to give us a hint that Ether was translated by the Lord? Or shall we conclude that Moroni, like most human beings, shows his interest in the last things which are said by a famous person?"[129]

Chapter Seventeen

CAIN

(Gen. 4; JST Gen. 5; Moses 5)

Though he is not classified as a translated being, we will discuss the cursed individual, Cain, who is still alive and was seen twice by Elder David W. Patten.[130] We begin by reading from the Old Testament:

"And Adam knew Eve his wife; and she conceived, *and bare Cain,* and said, I have gotten a man from the Lord. And she again bare his brother Abel. And Abel was a keeper of sheep, but *Cain was a tiller of the ground*" (Gen. 4: 1-2). (Italics added)

Because the Bible is an abridgement of sacred events, these scriptures have caused many to believe that these brothers were the first children born of Adam and Eve. However, from the *Pearl of Great Price,* we find out that prior to their births many "sons and daughters" were born to these righteous parents (Moses 5: 1-3).

Concerning Cain and Abel, we are informed from the Old Testament that "Cain brought of the fruit of the ground an offering unto the Lord. And Abel, he also brought of the firstlings of his flock and of the fat thereof. And the Lord had respect unto Abel and to his offering:

"*But unto Cain and to his offering he had not respect. And Cain was very wroth, and his countenance fell*" (Gen. 4: 3-5). (Italics added)

Considering Cain's offering, we find out from the *Pearl of Great Price* that "*Cain loved Satan more than God. And Satan commanded him, saying: Make an offering unto the Lord.* And in process of time it came to pass that Cain brought of the fruit of the ground an offering unto the Lord" (Moses 5: 18). (Italics added)

Why did Satan command Cain to make an offering to the Lord? Both Satan and Cain knew that the fruit of the ground was not the prescribed offering. Accordingly, both willfully displayed their disrespect and disobedience to the Lord. Regarding offerings, Elder Orson F. Whitney says:

> Adam's offering of sacrifice was acceptable to the Lord, being in accordance with the divine command, and because it truly symbolized the Lamb of God, who was to come. Abel, Adam's son, offered a similar sacrifice—"the firstlings of his flock and of the fat thereof, and the Lord had respect unto Abel and to his offering" (Gen. 4: 4). But Cain, Abel's eldest brother, who had also been taught the law of sacrifice, took it upon himself to deviate from the divine instruction, and instead of a lamb, he "brought of the fruit of the ground," an offering in no way typical of the Savior. Hence, his offering was rejected.[131]

"And the Lord said unto Cain: Why art thou wroth? Why is thy countenance fallen?" (Moses 5: 22). Without waiting for a response, the Lord gave this verbal warning:

"If thou doest well, thou shalt be accepted. *And if thou doest not well, sin lieth at the door*, and Satan desireth to have thee; and except thou shalt hearken unto my commandments, I will deliver thee up, and it shall be unto thee according to his desire." Then, the Lord added this interesting postscript: "*And thou shalt rule over him*" (Moses 5: 23). (Italics added)

Continuing, Jehovah spoke these somber words: "For from this time forth thou shalt be the father of his [Satan's] lies; thou shalt be called *Perdition*; for thou wast also before the world.

"And it shall be said in time to come—That these abominations were had from Cain; for he rejected the greater counsel which was had from God; *and this is a cursing which I will put upon thee*, except thou repent" (Moses 5: 24-25). (Italics added)

Because he loved Satan more than God, ". . . *Cain was wroth, and listened not any more to the voice of the Lord*, neither to Abel, his brother, who walked in holiness before the Lord" (Moses 5: 26). (Italics added)

Not only was Cain rebellious, we find out that some of his brothers were also disobedient: "And Adam and his wife mourned before the Lord, because of Cain and his brethren" (Moses 5: 27).

As time went on, "Cain took one of his [disobedient] brothers' daughters to wife, and they loved Satan more than God" (Moses 5: 28).

MASTER MAHAN

Some time after this marriage, Satan said to Cain:

"Swear unto me by thy throat, and if thou tell it thou shalt die; and swear thy [wayward] brethren by their heads, and by the living God, that they tell it not; for if they tell it, they shall surely die; and this that thy father [Adam] may not know it; and this day I will deliver thy brother Abel into thine hands" (Moses 5: 29).

Then, surprisingly, the Evil One made this solemn oath:

"*And Satan sware unto Cain that he would do according to his commands.* And all these things were done in secret. And Cain said: Truly I am Mahan, the master of this great secret, that I may murder and get gain. *Wherefore Cain was called Master Mahan*, and he gloried in his wickedness" (Moses 5: 30-31). (Italics added)

From Elder B. H. Roberts,[132] we gather this information:

". . . Satan's desires shall be towards Cain; He shall rejoice in Cain because the latter is a wicked man; and to win him completely to his kingdom Satan is even willing to abdicate his throne and consent for Cain to rule over him. All of which indicates the desperate wicked disposition of Cain before he reached the climax of his crimes in the murder of his brother, Abel."[133]

After killing his righteous brother, "Cain gloried in that which he had done, saying: I am free; surely the flocks of my brother falleth into my hands" (Moses 5: 33).

CAIN'S SIX CURSES
(Moses, *Teachings of the Prophet Joseph Smith*, pp. 58-59, 169)

Within a short time of Abel's murder, the Lord spoke to Cain and said: ". . . What hast thou done? The voice of thy brother's blood cries unto me from the ground. *And now thou shalt be cursed from the earth* which hath opened her mouth to receive thy brother's blood from thy hand" (5: 35-36). (Italics added)

Consequently, the Lord decreed a righteous judgment on Cain, who had cursed himself by committing a great sin. Again, we continue with the Lord's decree:

"When thou tillest the ground it shall not henceforth yield unto thee her strength. *A fugitive and a vagabond shalt thou be in the earth*" (5: 37). (Italics added)

Attempting to justify his actions, "Cain said unto the Lord: Satan tempted me because of my brother's flocks. And I was wroth also; for his offering thou didst accept and not mine; *my punishment is greater than I can bear.* Behold thou hast driven me out this day from the face of the Lord, and from thy face shall I be hid; and I shall be a fugitive and a vagabond in the earth; and it shall come to pass, that he that findeth me will slay me, because of mine iniquities, for these things are not hid from the Lord." (Italics added)

The Lord's response: "Whosoever slayeth thee, vengeance shall be taken on him sevenfold. And I the Lord set a mark upon Cain, lest any finding him should kill him."

From that time forward, ". . . Cain was shut out from the presence of the Lord, and with his wife and many of his brethren dwelt in the land of Nod, on the east of Eden" (5: 38-41).

Due to Cain's great iniquities, we learn that he brought upon himself six curses: (1) After tilling the ground, it would not yield unto him its abundance; (2) He was shut out from the presence of the Lord; (3) He was to be a fugitive and a vagabond in the earth; (4) He was cursed with a "mark" of dark skin; (5) He lost the Holy Priesthood; (6) Lastly, he was the first mortal to became a son of perdition.

CAIN VISITED ELDER DAVID W. PATTEN

When the Twelve Apostles were called in this dispensation, David W. Patten was the fifth member selected.[134] This noble soul was a man of great faith and dedication. Prior to being mortally wounded at the battle of Crooked River, Elder Patten met "a very remarkable personage." The following information is from Lycurgus A. Wilson's book on the life of David W. Patten:

It was probably not long after his arrival in Tennessee in the spring of 1836, that David had one of the most remarkable experiences of his life. He was making his home with Levi Taylor, the step-father of Abraham O. Smoot,[135] at the time and had been to Paris [Tennessee], some sixteen miles away, holding a meeting. Riding home in the evening, just where his road lay through a dense growth of brush, called in those part a 'barren,' he suddenly became aware that a person on foot by his side was keeping pace with the mule on which he rode.

But the subjoined letter, dated at Provo, Utah, will explain the matter:

President Joseph F. Smith, Salt Lake City, [Utah]:

Dear Brother:—In relation to the subject of the visit of Cain to Brother David W. Patten in the State of Tennessee, about which you wrote to me, I will say that according to the best of my recollection it was in the month of September, 1835.

It was in the evening, just twilight, when Brother Patten rode up to my father's house, alighted from his mule and came into the house. The family immediately observed that his countenance was quite changed. My mother having first noticed his changed appearance said: "Brother Patten, are you sick?" He replied that he was not, but had just met with a very remarkable personage who had represented himself as being Cain, who murdered his brother, Abel. He [Brother Patten] went on to tell the circumstances as near as I can recall in the following language:

As I was riding along the road on my mule I suddenly noticed a very strange personage walking besides me. He walked along beside me for about two miles. His head was about even with my shoulders as I sat in my saddle. He wore no clothing, but was covered with hair. His skin was very dark. I asked where he dwelt and he replied that he had no home, that he was a wanderer in the earth and traveled to and fro. He said he was a very miserable creature, that he had earnestly sought death during his sojourn upon the earth, but that he could not die, and his mission was to destroy the souls of men. About the time he expressed himself thus, I rebuked him in the name of the Lord Jesus Christ and by virtue of the Holy Priesthood, and commanded him to go hence, and he immediately departed out of my sight. When he left me I found myself near your house.

There was much conversation about the circumstances between Brother Patten and my family which I don't recall, but the above is in substance his statement to us at the time. The date is, to the best of my recollection, and I think it is correct, but it may [possibly] have been in the spring of 1836, but I feel quite positive that the former date is right.

Hoping the above will be satisfactory to you and answer your purpose, I am with the kindest regards, as ever,

Your friend and brother, A. O. Smoot.[136]

CAIN "A FUGITIVE AND A VAGABOND"

From what Cain told Elder Patten, we discover that his curse to be "a fugitive and a vagabond in the earth," meant he was doomed to travel to and fro upon the earth as a wanderer. Unlike the Three Nephites and John the Revelator, Cain did not desire to bring the souls of men unto Christ; in his own words, "his mission was to destroy the souls of men." Previously, we have read that the Three Nephites, (and undoubtedly John the Beloved) were given the promise, that they would not have pain while they dwelled in the flesh, "neither sorrow save it be for the sins of the world" (3 Ne. 28: 9). Unlike these translated beings, wicked Cain told Elder Patten "he was a very miserable creature." Therefore, his curse of being "a fugitive and a vagabond" was not a blessing, but a punishment. From Elder Abraham H. Cannon,[137] we read these comments about Cain:

"Brother J. F. Smith told about David Patten having seen and walked with Cain. Cain is described as being a very large man, his head being even with that of David Patten when the latter was seated on his animal. I always entertained the idea that Cain was dead, but my attention was called to the passage of scripture concerning the curse of God which should fall upon whoever should slay Cain (Moses 5: 40; Gen. 4: 15). I supposed this meant whoever should kill his seed."[138]

SECOND APPEARANCE OF CAIN

The following article was written by Henele Pikale and was printed in the *Juvenile Instructor*:

> *I visited Diahman in Daviess County [in June, 1838], and in company with the Prophet [Joseph Smith] and others went to see Adam's altar. It was in the timber, and where the stones came from, of which it was made I have no idea, as there was none like them in the country so far as I could learn. The stones of which it had been built were in huge blocks laying around near each other. In the afternoon of the same day, Brother George A. Smith and I went and bathed in Grand River, after which we went to the house of Lyman Wight, where the Prophet Joseph, Sidney Rigdon, Don Carlos Smith and David Patten were. Some of them killed a large rattle snake; they were looking at it, and here I heard Brother Patten say he had seen Cain, the murderer of Abel, as he was standing in a tent door . . .*[139]

According to the Prophet's history, he left in company with "Sidney Rigdon, Thomas B. Marsh, *David W. Patten,* Bishop Partridge, Elias Higbee, Simeon Carter, Alanson Ripley, *and many others,*" for the purpose of visiting the north country for various reasons. (Italics added)

On "Saturday, May 19, 1838," this party traveled to "Colonel Lyman Wight's home."[140] Therefore, it was in May, not June, when Elder Patten related the story of the second appearance of Cain.

A REASON FOR CAIN BEING ALIVE

If we might indulge in speculation, we would suggest a reason for Cain being alive: It has been written—"In the mouth of two or three witnesses shall every word be established" (2 Cor. 13: 1). Because John the Revelator and the Three Nephites desired to "bring the souls of men" unto Christ, they became righteous, translated beings. Thus, these *special witnesses* "minister unto all the scattered tribes of Israel, and unto all nations, kindreds, tongues and people, and shall bring out of them unto Jesus many souls, that their desires may be fulfilled, and also because of the convincing power of God which is in them" (3 Ne. 28: 29; D&C 7: 4-8).

Speaking to his son, Jacob, Lehi expounded this great doctrine: "*For it must needs be, that there is an opposition in all things.* If not so, my first-born in the wilderness, righteousness could not be brought to pass, neither wickedness, neither holiness nor misery, neither good nor bad. Wherefore, all things must needs be a compound in one . . ." (2 Ne. 2: 11). (Italics added)

Like Satan, Cain's work is "to destroy the souls of men." Therefore, Cain's mission upon this earth is in direct *opposition* to John the Revelator's and the Three Nephites' mission of bringing the souls of men unto Christ (3 Ne. 28: 9; D&C 7: 4-8).

Regarding Cain's statement to Elder Patten "that he could not die," a valid question may be asked: How did Cain survive the flood in Noah's day? From the scriptures, we are informed that only "eight souls" were saved (Gen. 7; Heb. 11: 7; 1 Peter 3: 20). We answer—the Lord has not revealed this information. Perhaps Cain was taken from the earth during that time? From Elder Patten, we know that Cain is alive and travels to and fro upon the earth as a wanderer, seeking to destroy the souls of men.

NOTE

1. David W. Patten was ordained an apostle on February 15, 1835, under the hands of Oliver Cowdery, David Whitmer, and Martin Harris, at age 35; he was killed on October 25, 1838, at the Battle of Crooked River, Missouri, at age 38.

2. Brigham H. Roberts was sustained as one of the First Seven Presidents of the Seventy on October 7, 1888, at age 31; he then was set apart by Lorenzo Snow; he died on September 27, 1933, at Salt Lake City, Utah, at age 76.

3. Abraham O. Smoot was a faithful member of the Church, who is mentioned several times in the *Documentary History of the Church*. See the following Volumes and pages for more information: 3: 347; 4: 12, 403; 6: 150, 338; 7: 129, 548, 555, and 629.

4. Abraham H. Cannon was sustained as one of the First Seven Presidents of the Seventy on October 8, 1882, at age 23; ordained an apostle on October 7, 1889, by Joseph F. Smith, at age 30; he died on July 19, 1896, at Salt Lake City, Utah, at age 37.

Chapter Eighteen

The Purpose for Translated Beings

(JST Gen. 14: 32; Moses 7: 27)

From what has been presented in this work, we have found that from the days of Enoch to the time of the flood, new converts and true believers, except those people who were needed to carry out the Lord's purposes on the earth, were translated and taken up into heaven. After the flood, except in a few special cases—those of Moses, Elijah, John the Beloved, Alma the son of Alma, Nephi the son of the third Helaman, and the Three Nephites—each involving a special purpose, the Lord ceased translating faithful people.

Concerning John the Beloved and the Three Nephites, it is proper to wonder what the purpose was for these translated beings remaining on the earth until the second coming of Christ. It is this author's belief that there are four reasons for their presence upon the earth. First: Due to their great faith and desire, the Lord allowed them to become translated beings, for the main purpose of bringing the souls of men unto Christ (3 Ne. 28: 9, 29: D&C 7: 2). Secondly: They are performing great and marvelous works before the judgment day of the Lord (3 Ne. 28: 31-33). Thirdly: Cain is still alive. Having a tangible body, he has special abilities to travel to and fro upon the earth, seeking to destroy the souls of men. Being in opposition to Cain, John the Beloved and the Three Nephites have a tangible body, with special abilities to move over the earth, bringing the souls of men unto Christ.

For the fourth purpose why John the Beloved and the Three Nephites are alive, we turn to the expressions of Elder Harold B. Lee:

> President [J. Reuben] Clark[141] said something that startled some folks years ago. He said, "It is my faith that the gospel plan has always been here, that His priesthood has always been here, that His priesthood has been here on the earth, and that it will continue to be so until the end comes." When that conference session was over there were many who said, "My goodness, doesn't President Clark realize that there have been periods of apostasy following each dispensation of the gospel?"
>
> I walked over to the Church Office Building with President Joseph Fielding Smith and he said, "I believe there has never been a moment of time since the creation but what there has been someone holding the priesthood on the earth to hold Satan in check." And then I thought of Enoch's city with perhaps thousands who were taken into heaven and were translated. They must have been translated for a purpose and may have sojourned with those living on the earth ever since that time. I have thought of Elijah—and perhaps Moses, for all we know; they were translated beings, as was John the Revelator. I have thought of the three Nephites. Why were they translated and permitted to tarry? For

what purpose? An answer was suggested when I heard President Smith, whom we have considered one of our well-informed theologians, make the above statement. Now that doesn't mean that the kingdom of God has always been present, because these men did not have the authority to administer the saving ordinances of the gospel to the world. But these individuals were translated for a purpose known to the Lord. There is no question but what they were here.[142]

Concerning the apostasy, Elder Smith, himself, has written this explanation: "There has never been a time from the beginning when the influence of the Spirit of the Lord has not been active on the face of the earth . . ."[143] Two pages later, he quoted this revelation given to the Prophet Joseph Smith: "'Wherefore, I will that all men shall repent, for all are under sin, *except those which I have reserved unto myself, holy men that ye know not of*' (D&C 49: 5-8). Continuing, he says: "There are several important prophets who were granted the privilege of remaining on the earth. John the Revelator was one of these . . . Elijah evidently was another . . . The scriptural inference is that Moses also was translated as was Alma . . ."[144] (Italics added)

From the expressions of Elders Lee and Smith, we know that these translated beings served an important purpose upon this earth. And as has been discussed in this work, John the Beloved and the Three Nephites will continue to serve a special purpose upon this earth, until the Lord's second coming.

"WHAT DOES THE FUTURE HOLD
FOR THE NEPHITE LEGEND?"

Though a few stories mention the appearance of John the Beloved, the majority of the narratives that are housed in folklore archives, located at various universities, mention the appearance of one or more of the Three Nephites.

In a very informative article that was written by Professor William A. Wilson,[145] he asks and answers the following question:

> *What does the future hold for the Nephite legend? Will the old stories continue to be told, and will we still hear about new ones? Or in our supposedly more sophisticated age, will the stories eventually disappear?*
>
> *To answer these questions, we must ask still others: Will Mormons continue to hold fast to the visions of Joseph Smith? Will they continue to believe that God personally leads the Church, rewarding the faithful and punishing sinners? Will Church members continue to seek evidence of God's participation in their daily affairs, and will they continue to tell others about this participation? So long as answers to these questions remain affirmative, the Nephite stories will probably remain. Or if they do disappear, they will be replaced by similar stories that meet similar needs in the lives of those who tell and believe them.*
>
> *What we must remember is that the Nephite accounts are really only a small part of a much larger body of Mormon supernatural lore that shows no signs of diminishing—a lore generated by belief in a personal*

God who actively intervenes in people's lives. And this
lore speaks to the same central issues as those reflected
in the Nephite narratives—genealogy work, temple
work, missionary work, personal worthiness, and
divine help in solving personal problems. In fact, the
Nephite stories are so similar in subject matter to the
rest of Mormon lore that stories often slip easily from
one genre to another.[146]

Continuing his evaluation, Brother Wilson says: "Some may argue that the stories will continue for still another reason—because they are true. If the Book of Mormon is really the word of God, the following Book of Mormon description of the Three Nephites ought to be sufficient explanation for the continuance of the stories: 'And they are as the angels of God, and . . . can show themselves unto whatsoever man it seemeth them good. Therefore, great and marvelous works shall be wrought by them, before the great and coming day [of judgment]' (3 Ne. 28: 30-31)."[147]

By way of testimony, Brother Wilson adds these comments: "But as a Latter-day Saint who believes in the Book of Mormon, I also believe that the Three Nephites may do what the Book of Mormon says they can do. Having read hundreds of Nephite accounts and having compared them with each other, with Mormon folklore in general, and with supernatural legends outside Mormon tradition, I can discount many of the narratives. But I can't discount them all."[148]

From what has been written in this work, I, too, add my testimony that God lives, and Jesus is the Christ. That Joseph Smith is a prophet of God, who translated the *Book of Mormon* by the power of God. I further declare by the power of the Holy Ghost that John the Beloved and the Three Nephites still minister upon this earth, for the main purpose of bringing the souls of men unto Christ. And as many stories have affirmed, they can show themselves unto whomever they desire. Therefore, individually and collectively, these special, translated men will perform great and marvelous works, before the second coming of our Lord (3 Ne. 28: 30-31).

NOTE

1. J. Reuben Clark, Jr. was sustained as Second Counselor to President Heber J. Grant on April 6, 1933, at age 61; sustained as First Counselor to President Grant on October 6, 1934; ordained an apostle, October 11, 1934, at age 63, by President Grant; sustained as First Counselor to President George Albert Smith on May 21, 1945; sustained as Second Counselor to President David O. McKay on April 9, 1951; sustained as First Counselor to President McKay on June 12, 1959; he died on October 6, 1961, at Salt Lake City, Utah, at age 90.

2. William A. Wilson, professor of English and Scandinavian, was the chairman of the BYU English department and director of the BYU Folklore Archives. He has published widely on various topics.

CHAPTER ONE

1 See Note 1 at end of chapter.

2 Dr. Sidney B. Sperry, *The Book of Mormon Testifies*, Bookcraft, Fourth Edition, 1960, p. 315. Used by permission.

3 Ibid., p. 316.Used by permission.

4 Ibid., p. 294. Used by permission.

5 Ibid., p. 294. Used by permission.

6 See Note 2 at end of chapter

7 Bruce R. McConkie, *The Mortal Messiah: From Bethlehem to Calvary*, Book 4, Deseret Book, 1985, pp. 306-307. Used by permission.

8 See the author's books, *Mary, Mother of Jesus*, pp. 47-48, and *Simon Peter*, p. 220.

CHAPTER TWO

9 Dr. Sidney B. Sperry, *The Book of Mormon Testifies*, Bookcraft, Fourth Edition, 1960, Footnote 5, p. 295. Used by permission.

10 See Note 1 at end of chapter.

11 *Documentary History of the Church*, Volume 4, p. 538. Used by permission.

12 See Note 2 at end of chapter.

13 Joseph Fielding Smith, *Answers to Gospel Questions*, Volume 1, Deseret Book, 1957, p. 122. Used by permission.

14 Bruce R. McConkie, *The Millennial Messiah: The Second Coming of the Son of Man*, Deseret Book, 1982, p. 680. Used by permission.

15 Dr. Sidney B. Sperry, *The Book of Mormon Testifies*, Bookcraft, Fourth Edition, 1960, p. 305. Used by permission.

16 See Note 3 at end of chapter.

17 President Joseph F. Smith, An address given at Ogden, Utah, Sunday

morning, June 21, 1883, as recorded in the *Journal of Discourses*, Volume 24, p. 191.

18 Joseph Fielding Smith, *Answers to Gospel Questions*, Volume 3, Deseret Book, 1960, p. 39. Used by permission.

19 Ibid., pp. 39-40. Used by permission.

20 Ibid., p. 40. Used by permission.

21 Dr. Sidney B. Sperry, *The Book of Mormon Testifies*, Bookcraft, Fourth Edition, 1960, p. 306. Used by permission.

22 See Note 4 at the end of chapter.

23 James E. Talmage, *Jesus the Christ*, 1962 ed., p. 744.

24 Joseph Fielding Smith, *Answers to Gospel Questions*, Volume 1, Deseret Book, 1957, p. 124. Used by permission.

25 Bruce R. McConkie, *The Mortal Messiah: From Bethlehem to Calvary*, Book 4, Deseret Book, 1981, p. 301. Used by permission.

26 Ibid., pp. 301-302. Used by permission.

Chapter Three

27 This same information is in the author's book, *Simon Peter*, pp. 95-98.

28 This same information is in the author's book, *Simon Peter*, p. 43-46.

29 James E. Talmage, *Jesus the Christ*, 1962 ed., p. 228.

30 Bruce R. McConkie, *The New Witness of the Articles of Faith*, Deseret Book, 1985, pp. 348-349. Used by permission.

31 Ibid., p. 349. Used by permission.

32 Ibid., p. 349. Used by permission.

33 Ibid., pp. 349-350. Used by permission.

34 Bruce R. McConkie, *Doctrinal New Testament Commentary, Volume 1, The Gospels*, Bookcraft, 1965, p. 133. Used by permission.

35 Bruce R. McConkie, *Mormon Doctrine*, 2nd ed., Bookcraft, 1966, p. 651. Used by permission.

CHAPTER FOUR

36 Dr. Sidney B. Sperry, *The Book of Mormon Testifies*, Bookcraft, Fourth Edition, 1960, p. 297. Used by permission.

CHAPTER FIVE

37 Bruce R. McConkie, *The Mortal Messiah: From Bethlehem to Calvary*, Book 4, Deseret Book, 1981, p. 389. Used by permission.
38 See the author's book, *Simon Peter*, pp. 224-225.
39 James E. Talmage, *Jesus the Christ*, 1962 ed., p. 694.
40 Bruce R. McConkie, *The Mortal Messiah: From Bethlehem to Calvary*, Book 4, Deseret Book, 1981, p. 390. Used by permission.
41 Ibid., pp. 390-391. Used by permission.
42 See Note 1 at end of chapter.
43 President Heber C. Kimball, An address given in the Bowery, Salt Lake City, Utah, as recorded in the *Journal of Discourses*, Volume 10, p. 101.
44 See Note 2 at end of chapter.
45 Elder Wilford Woodruff, An address given in the Tabernacle, Salt Lake City, Utah, as recorded in the *Journal of Discourses*, Volume 18, p. 191.
46 Bruce R. McConkie, *A New Witness for the Articles of Faith*, Deseret Book, 1985, pp. 200-201. Used by permission.

CHAPTER SIX

47 Bruce R. McConkie, *Mormon Doctrine*, 2nd ed., 1966, Bookcraft, p. 803. Used by permission.
48 Bruce R. McConkie, *The Mortal Messiah: From Bethlehem to Calvary*, Book 4, Deseret Book, 1981, p. 394. Used by permission.
49 See Note 1 at end of chapter.
50 Elder Franklin D. Richards, An address given in the Logan

Tabernacle, May 17, 1884, as recorded in the *Journal of Discourses*, Volume 25, pp. 236-237.

51 An address of President Wilford Woodruff, who then was President of the Quorum of the Twelve Apostles, given May 20, 1882, as recorded in the *Deseret News Weekly* 31: 334, No. 21, June 14, 1882.

52 *A Comprehensive History of the Church*, Volume 6, pp. 354-355. Used by permission.

53 James E. Talmage, *Jesus the Christ*, 1962 ed., p. 739.

54 *Documentary History of the Church,* Volume 5, pp. 347-349. Used by permission.

55 Bruce R. McConkie, *The Mortal Messiah: From Bethlehem to Calvary*, Book 4, Deseret Book, 1981, pp. 395-396. Used by permission.

CHAPTER SEVEN

56 Joseph Fielding Smith, comp., *Teachings of the Prophet Joseph Smith*, 1938, p. 170.

57 Ibid., p. 170.

58 Elder Wilford Woodruff, An address given at the New Tabernacle, at Salt Lake City, Utah, on September 5, 1869, as recorded in the *Journal of Discourses*, Volume 13, p. 320.

59 Joseph Fielding Smith, comp., *Teachings of the Prophet Joseph Smith*, 1938, p. 171.

60 See Note 1 at end of chapter.

61 Elder Orson Pratt, An address given at the Old Tabernacle, in Salt Lake City, Utah, on July 19, 1874, as recorded in the *Journal of Discourses*, Volume 17, p. 147.

62 Bruce R. McConkie, *The Millennial Messiah*, Deseret Book, 1982, p. 644. Used by permission.

63 See Note 2 at end of chapter.

64 President Brigham Young, An address given at the Tabernacle, at Salt Lake City, Utah, on June 5, 1859, as recorded in the *Journal of*

Discourses, Volume 7, p. 163. See also the author's book, *Mysteries of the Kingdom*, p. 63.

65 See Note 3 at end of chapter.

66 Charles W. Penrose, *"Mormon"Doctrine, Plain and Simple, or Leaves from the Tree of Life*. Published 1888, p. 44. See also the author's book, *Mysteries of the Kingdom*, pp. 63-64.

67 Bruce R. McConkie, *The Millennial Messiah*, Deseret Book, 1982, p. 644. Used by permission.

68 See Note 4 at end of chapter.

69 President Anthony W. Ivins, Second Counselor to President Heber J. Grant, Lecture No. 20, July 6, 1921, *The Book of Mormon as an Evidence of the Divinity of Mormonism*, p. 3. In the LDS Church Archives PQ M266.04 S471.

70 See Note 5 at end of chapter.

71 Elder Melvin J. Ballard, an address titled, *The Path to Celestial Happiness*, spoken in the Tabernacle in Salt Lake City, Utah, on October 25, 1925, as printed in *The Deseret News*, October 31, 1925. See also *Masterpieces of Latter-Saint Leaders*, by N.B. Lundwall, p. 99.

CHAPTER EIGHT

72 Oliver B. Huntington, His Personal History, pp. 5-6, which is housed at a special collection library at Brigham Young University.

73 *Documentary History of the Church*, Volume 3, pp. 187-188, dated October 30-31, 1838. Used by permission.

74 Oliver B. Huntington, His Personal History, pp. 5-6, which is housed at a special collection library at Brigham Young University.

75 *A Comprehensive History of The Church*, Volume 1, p. 484. Used by permission.

76 E. S., *Millennial Star*, 49: 254, April 18, 1887.

77 *Doctrines And Covenants Commentary*, Revised Edition, 1965, p. 508. Used by permission. See also *The Historical Record*, Vol. 6, Numbers 3-5, May 1887, pp. 208-209.

78 Amasa Porter, *Labors in the Vineyard*, pp. 80-81, *Faith-promoting Series*, number 12, 1884. This series was published by The Juvenile Instructor Office in Salt Lake City, Utah, in 1884, and consisted of 17 volumes.

CHAPTER NINE

79 Elder Orson Pratt, An address given in the new Bowery, at Salt Lake City, Utah, on April 7, 1855, as recorded in the *Journal of Discourses*, Vol. 2, p. 264.

80 Elder Orson Pratt, An address given in the new Tabernacle, at Salt Lake City, Utah, on April 11, 1875, as recorded in the *Journal of Discourses*, Volume 18, pp. 19-20.

81 See Note 1 at end of chapter.

82 Elder Orson F. Whitney, Council of the Twelve, *Through Memory Halls*, an autobiography of Elder Whitney, Zion's Printing and Publishing Company, Independence, Missouri, 1930, pp. 260-261.

83 See Note 2 at end of chapter.

84 *Heber J. Grant, Man of Steel, Prophet of God*, by Francis M. Gibbons, Deseret Book, Salt Lake City, First Printing, 1979, pp. 114, 116. Used by permission.

85 Elder Heber J. Grant, *Heber J. Grant Journal and Letter Extracts* from February 14, 1901 thru September 8, 1903, pp. 18-19.

86 See Note 3 at end of chapter.

87 See Note 4 at end of chapter.

88 LeGrand Richards, *Israel! Do You Know*, Deseret Book Company, 1954, pp. 229-230. Used by permission.

89 Ibid., p. 230. Used by permission.

90 Ibid., pp. 232. Used by permission.

91 Ibid., pp. 232-233. Used by permission.

92 Ibid., p. 233. Used by permission.

93 See Note 5 at end of chapter.

94 President Harold B. Lee, Mexico Conference Report, August 27, 1972, p. 118. Used by permission.

CHAPTER TEN

95 Bruce R. McConkie, *The Millennial Messiah*, Deseret Book, 1982, p. 284.

96 Ibid., p. 285. Used by permission.

97 President Brigham Young, An address given in the Tabernacle, at Salt Lake City, Utah, June 3, 1860, as recorded in the *Journal of Discourses*, Volume 8, p. 279.

98 President Heber C. Kimball, First Counselor to President Brigham Young, An address in the Tabernacle, Salt Lake City, Utah, given August 13, 1853, as recorded in the *Journal of Discourses*, Volume 2, p. 105.

99 President Heber C. Kimball, First Counselor to President Brigham Young, An address given November 19, 1854, as printed in *The Deseret News*, Vol. 4, p. 147, No. 40, December 14, 1854.

100 Elder Wilford Woodruff, "His Daily Journal," March 30, 1873.

101 See Note 1 at end of chapter.

102 President George Q. Cannon, First Counselor to President John Taylor, An article written in *The Juvenile Instructor*, 19: 184, printed June 15, 1884.

103 Leon M. Strong, *Three Timely Treasures*, Zion's Printing & Publishing Co., Independence, Missouri, 1949, p. 32.

104 Orson Pratt, Council of the Twelve, *The Seer*, pp. 263-264, Washington D.C. Edition, May 1854.

105 Elder Harold B. Lee, An address given July 8, 1964, as printed in *Stand Ye in Holy Places, Selected sermons and writings of President Harold B. Lee*, Deseret Book, 1974, p. 161. Used by permission.

Chapter Eleven

106 Bruce R. McConkie, *The Millennial Messiah*, Deseret Book, 1982, p. 297. Used by permission.

107 Ibid., p. 284. Used by permission.

108 Ibid., p. 285. Used by permission.

Chapter Twelve

109 See the author's book, *Simon Peter*, pp. 142-144.

110 Charles W. Penrose, An address given June 25, 1893, as printed in the *Millennial Star*, 55: 559, dated August 28, 1893.

111 President Brigham Young, An address given in the Tabernacle, June 19, 1859, Salt Lake City, Utah, as recorded in the *Journal of Discourses*, Volume 6, p. 133 and Volume 7, p. 193.

112 *Doctrines of Salvation, Sermons and Writings of Joseph Fielding Smith*, Compiled by Bruce R. McConkie, Volume 2, Bookcraft, 1955, p. 107. Used by permission.

113 Ibid., pp. 110-111. Used by permission.

114 Ibid., p. 111. Used by permission.

Chapter Thirteen

115 See the author's book, *Simon Peter*, pp. 224-225.

116 James E. Talmage, *Jesus the Christ*, 1962 ed., p. 694.

117 Wilford Woodruff, An address given in the new Tabernacle, Salt Lake City, Utah, September 5, 1869, as recorded in the *Journal of Discourses*, Volume 13, p. 320.

118 Oliver B. Huntington, His Personal History, p. 5, which is housed at a special collection library at Brigham Young University.

119 *Documentary History of the Church*, Volume 2, p. 73. Used by permission.

120 Ibid., p. 73. Used by permission.

121 Ibid., Volume 1, p. 176. Used by permission.

CHAPTER FOURTEEN

122 Dr. Sidney B. Sperry, *The Book of Mormon Testifies*, Bookcraft, Fourth Edition, 1960, pp. 197-198. Used by permission.

123 Joseph Fielding Smith, *Answers to Gospel Questions*, Volume 5, Deseret Book, 1966, p. 38. Used by permission.

124 Bruce R. McConkie, *Mormon Doctrine*, 2nd ed., Bookcraft, 1966, p. 805. Used by permission.

CHAPTER FIFTEEN

125 See Note 1 at end of chapter.

126 Bruce R. McConkie, *The Mortal Messiah: From Bethlehem to Calvary*, Book 1, Deseret Book, 1979, pp. 413-414. Used by permission. See also the author's book, Mary, Mother of Jesus, p. 42.

127 Dr. Sidney B. Sperry, *The Book of Mormon Testifies*, Bookcraft, Fourth Edition, 1960, p. 285. Used by permission.

CHAPTER SIXTEEN

128 Dr. Sidney B. Sperry, *The Book of Mormon Testifies*, Bookcraft, Fourth Edition, 1960, pp. 348-349, 370. Used by permission.

129 Ibid., p. 370. Used by permission.

CHAPTER SEVENTEEN

130 See Note 1 at end of chapter.

131 Elder Orson F. Whitney, Gospel Themes, p. 100, December, 1913.

132 See Note 2 at end of chapter.

133 Elder B. H. Roberts, First Council of Seventy, The Seventy's Course in Theology, Second Year, 1908, pp. 60-61.

134 *Documentary History of the Church*, Volume 2, p. 187. Used by permission.See also Joseph Fielding Smith, Essentials in Church

History, Nineteenth Edition, 1964, Deseret Book, p. 181.

135 See Note 3 at end of chapter.

136 Lycurgus A. Wilson, *Life of David W. Patten,The First Apostolic Martyr*, Copyrighted 1900, 1904 Edition, The Deseret News, Salt Lake City, Utah, pp. 45-47. Other references: *The Miracle of Forgiveness*, pp. 127-128, *The Juvenile Instructor*, 21: 38; *Millennial Star*, 56: 382.

137 See Note 4 at end of chapter.

138 Abraham H. Cannon, his daily journal, November 9, 1893, p. 26.

139 Henele Pikale, *The Juvenile Instructor* 21: 38, February 1, 1886.

140 *Documentary History of the Church*, Volume 3, pp. 34-35. Used by permission.

CHAPTER EIGHTEEN

141 See Note 1 at end of chapter.

142 *Stand Ye in Holy Places, Selected Sermons and writings of President Harold B. Lee*, Deseret Book, 1975, pp. 161-162. Used by permission.

143 Joseph Fielding Smith, *Answers to Gospel Questions*, Volume 5, Deseret Book, 1966, p. 37. Used by permission.

144 Ibid., pp. 36-38. Used by permission.

145 See Note 2 at end of chapter.

146 William A. Wilson, *Freeways, Parking Lots, and Ice Cream Stands: The Three Nephites in Contemporary Society*, as printed in Dialogue—A Journal of Mormon Thought, Vol. 21, No. 3, Autumn 1988, p. 23. Used by permission.

147 Ibid., p. 24. Used by permission.

148 Ibid., p. 24. Used by permission.

Index

About the Author

The author, Bruce E. Dana, is an avid student of the gospel, who is a returned missionary with service in the Northwestern States and Pacific Northwest missions for the Church. He attended Weber State College and Utah State University. For several years, he was a mortgage banker. He has also worked for both the county and federal government, and is presently employed as a coordinator.

Brother Dana has served in a wide variety of Church callings, and enjoys teaching the doctrines of the gospel. He is married to Brenda Lamb, and is the father of eight children.

9 26575 76879 7